# Christianity
# in the Modern World

# CHRISTIANITY
## IN THE MODERN WORLD

## David Field

*Vice-Principal of Oak Hill College*

## Hulton Educational

*Photo Acknowledgements*
The publishers wish to thank the following for permission to use copyright photographs:
John Topham Picture Library: 21, 33, 97 (both), 119, 133 (John Topham/Jane Burton), 150; Salvation Army: 27, 71; Richard Gardner: 53; Central Office of Information: 77, 105; World Health Organisation: 141 (both).

*First published in Great Britain* 1983
*by* Hulton Educational Publications Ltd
Old Station Drive, Leckhampton, Cheltenham GL53 0DN

Reprinted 1983, 1984, 1985, 1986

ISBN 0 7175 0974 5

Printed and bound in Great Britain
at the Bath Press, Avon

# Contents

|  | Page |
|---|---|
| *Part A. Having standards* | |
| 1. Are standards out of date? | 9 |
| 2. Love and rules | 16 |
| *Part B. Personal relationships* | |
| 3. Family life | 23 |
| 4. Sex and sexism | 30 |
| 5. Friendship, love and marriage | 36 |
| 6. Divorce | 42 |
| *Part C. Work and leisure* | |
| 7. Finding a job | 48 |
| 8. Attitudes to work | 55 |
| 9. Attitudes to money | 60 |
| 10. Attitudes to leisure | 66 |
| *Part D. Society's casualties* | |
| 11. Community service | 73 |
| 12. Addiction | 80 |
| 13. Race and colour | 86 |
| 14. Crime and punishment | 92 |
| 15. Unwanted life | 99 |
| *Part E. Society's structures* | |
| 16. Politics | 107 |
| 17. Censorship and freedom | 114 |
| 18. Relationships at work | 122 |
| 19. Ecology and conservation | 128 |
| *Part F. World affairs* | |
| 20. World poverty | 136 |
| 21. War and peace | 144 |
| 22. Human rights | 151 |

# Preface

If you throw a stone into a pond, the ripples spread outwards from the splash. This book has been written rather like that. It begins with personal values, and the difficult business of making one's own decisions about right and wrong. Then it moves outwards to consider relationships with others at home and at work. Finally, it reaches the edge of the 'world pond', with sections on social and international issues.

Writing the book has been a family effort. My son Stephen made up the questions at the end of each chapter, and my daughter Carolyn did all the typing. They both go to Southgate School in North London.

One of my main aims has been to relate modern life to the Bible's teaching. The quotations from the biblical text usually come from the *Good News Bible* or the *New International Version*.

David Field

*Part A*

# Having standards

---

## 1. Are standards out of date?

'Oh dear', sighs father from his place in front of the television. 'In my young days tennis players didn't argue with umpires at Wimbledon. Standards are certainly slipping.' 'Slipping, my foot!' snorts grandma, clicking her knitting kneedles furiously. 'They've slipped already. I got on the bus with all my shopping yesterday, and no-one offered me a seat.'

Have standards dropped? Some certainly have. But others are held more strongly today than ever before. Take racism, for example. In grandma's day, very few people would have raised their voices against the principle of apartheid, but modern consciences are far more tender. If a black demonstrator from a South African township dies in police custody tomorrow, there will be a world outcry in a matter of hours.

Even those who say they have no standards at all turn out to have some very strong ideas about right and wrong when you question them closely. A car thief may get very angry if you kick his dog. And a rapist may be a very keen blood donor. Everyone has standards of some kind.

When people say that moral standards are slipping, they usually mean one of two things. They either mean that modern people are no longer willing to accept *old* standards. Or they mean that other people are not willing to accept *their* standards. Let us explore further and find out why this should be so.

**Impatience with standards**

(i) *Authority.* The day young Winston Churchill started at a new school, he was told to do a Latin exercise. 'Why?' he asked. There was an amazed silence. Finally, controlling his anger, the teacher replied 'Because I told you to do it!'

Gone are the days when any person in authority can issue an order like that without being expected to give a good reason for it. From their first weeks in primary school, children are encouraged nowadays to ask the question 'Why?'. And sometimes the answers adults get, when they ask society's figures of authority the same question, leave them unsatisfied.

Many people today mistrust those who make and enforce the laws. They listen to party political broadcasts cynically, because they suspect the politicians' motives. They read about police corruption in their daily papers, and their confidence in the whole police force is shaken. And when an archbishop or the Pope speaks out about moral standards on television, they shrug their shoulders and say, 'So what?'

In the rest of this book there will be frequent references to the Bible's teaching. That is partly because the syllabus requires you to know about it, but mainly because this is a book about *Christianity* in the modern world, and Christians accept the authority of the Bible. Nevertheless, the Bible's authority is under attack, too.

When a man is ordained into the ministry of the Church of England, he is asked 'Do you accept the Holy Scriptures as revealing all things necessary for eternal salvation through faith in Jesus Christ?', and he has to reply, 'I do so accept them.' But if he strides through his parish, laying down the law on moral issues, and answering all questions by thundering 'Because the Bible says so', he will not get very far with most people! Why should they be asked to accept the authority of a book written thousands of years ago? We would not think of working from an ancient textbook in physics or chemistry, so why should we do it in R.E.?

One reason, then, why old standards are threatened today is that all sources of authority are being questioned. Modern people are reluctant to accept any rules or principles that have simply been handed down to them from the past. They prefer to work things out for themselves.

(ii) *Responsibility.*   No-one can be held morally responsible for doing something unless he or she is capable of *not* doing it. That may sound complicated, but it is one of the fundamental principles on which the law of the land rests. If a man kills his wife, he cannot be convicted of murder if he is proved to be insane. The court may be satisfied that he is the culprit, but they cannot hold him responsible if he is mentally sick.

The same principle applies to keeping moral standards. I may do something that is obviously wrong (such as shoplifting), but I cannot be blamed if I could not help doing it (if, for example, I am a kleptomaniac). Blaming someone for failing to keep a standard he or she could never keep is as silly as blaming a friend with flu for having a high temperature!

The standards the Bible sets for moral living are very high, but until quite recently it was generally assumed that any sane person could achieve them — if not *always*, then at least some of the time. I may have told a lie yesterday, but I need not have done it. You may be in the grip of a bad habit today, but you could break it.

For some time now, however, behaviourists have been trying to persuade us that our patterns of behaviour are fixed, completely beyond our control. If certain principles are drummed into our heads in early childhood, they say, we will form outlooks and habits which we shall never be able to break. So when someone blames us for failing to live up to biblical (or any other) standards, we can answer: 'I'm sorry, but I can't help it. Don't blame me, blame my upbringing and the pressures of my environment.'

Here, then, is a second threat to standards. Having any standard only makes sense if you can reach it. If it is beyond your reach, because your patterns of behaviour and your attitudes are fixed by forces beyond your control, it is senseless to try to keep it.

(iii) *Deciding by results.* A third reason why many people are cutting loose from old moral standards turns the spotlight on to the way moral decisions are made. Putting it at its simplest, there are three main ways in which a person can come to a moral judgement.

The first way is to take the *rules route.* All you need there is a book of rules you can trust, one that is full enough to tell you the difference between right and wrong in difficult cases. When you need to make a decision, you just look up the problem in the index of your rule book, find the right page, and read off the answer.

When people talk about standards, they usually mean moral

rules. Dropping your standards means breaking the rules. If you take a purse you find on the floor of the supermarket instead of handing it in, you have lowered the standard of honesty by breaking the rule that says, 'You must not steal'.

A second way to make a moral decision is to take the *motives route*. This means that you are keener to ask the question 'Why?' than the question 'What?'. If you catch a man stealing in a supermarket, you may turn a blind eye to what he has done and try to find out why he has done it. Was it prompted by sheer greed? If so, the motive was bad and the offender should be punished. But you may find that he had no money and was stealing food from the shelves in order to support a starving family. If you were satisfied that his motives were thoroughly good, you might excuse his action (whatever the rule book said), and even help him to escape undetected.

The third way to moral decision-making is the *results route*. Using this method means that you are less interested in discovering what was done and why it was done than in finding out what happened afterwards.

Many people today take this third route in making their moral decisions. If you can prove that a certain act of stealing (or anything else) did more harm than good, they will agree that it was wrong. But for the same reason they will argue that Robin Hood was absolutely right to steal from the rich, because in his case a great many poor people received help as a result, while his victims hardly noticed what they had lost.

It is easy to see how the *motives route* (to some extent) and the *results route* (to a greater extent) lead away from traditional standards. If you follow either of these routes in making moral decisions, you will be impatient with those who claim that standards are falling, just because moral rules have been broken.

## A Christian perspective

Christians would agree with many of these points. Jesus himself criticized those who made all their moral decisions by the 'rules route' (the Scribes and Pharisees). The New Testament agrees that outside influences can strongly affect the way people behave. It also sharply challenges figures of authority (important people) who lay down standards without believing in them.

Nevertheless, Christians believe that standards are vitally

important. We can begin to see why, if we look again at the questions of *authority*, *responsibility* and routes to *decision-making*.

(i) *Authority.* It is one of the basic features of the Christian faith that God's authority can be trusted and must be obeyed. 'No one is good', said Jesus, 'but God alone.' (*Mark* 10:18). 'The will of God', writes Paul, is 'what is good and acceptable and perfect.' (*Romans* 12:2). Whether you believe that principle or not is a matter of personal faith, of course. But there can be no doubt that it is central in Christian teaching about morality.

Here, then, is the big difference between the Christian view of authority and others. Many figures of authority say, 'Do what I tell you.' They may be questioned and criticized. A few important people go further and dare to say, 'Do as I do.' But their standards could be wrong. God goes further still. He says, 'Be as I am' (see *Matthew* 5:48). And, in the Christian view, He alone has the right to make that claim, because He alone is good.

This approach to authority explains why Christians give such weight to the Bible's teaching. The Bible, they believe, explains God's goodness and sets out his will. It is far more than a book of rules. If it were just that, it would soon have become out of date and useless. But because it deals with things that time cannot change, especially God's nature and human nature, its impact is always fresh and up-to-date.

(ii) *Responsibility.* Christians go along with modern behaviourists in recognizing the enormous pressures that influence the way ordinary people behave. The Old Testament stresses the vital part that family background and upbringing play in moral decision-making (see *Ezekiel* 18:2). The Bible also makes much of the deep-seated tendency in human nature to rebel against right standards of behaviour. No-one describes the battles that go on in many people's consciences more vividly than Paul, when he writes, 'I know that good does not live in me — that is, in my human nature. For even though the desire to do good is in me, I am not able to do it. I don't do the good I want to do; instead, I do the evil that I do not want to do.' (*Romans* 7:18–19).

Nevertheless, Christians cannot agree with behaviourists who say that each of us is completely at the mercy of these powerful influences. One of the biggest claims of the Christian gospel is that any believer, however weak, has God's resources to overcome those pressures. Again, it is Paul who spells it out most clearly: 'God is always at work in you to make you willing and able to obey His own purpose.' (*Philippians* 2:13).

This extra 'God factor' strengthens the place of right standards by underlining people's responsibility to keep them. If a standard cannot be reached, no-one can be blamed for not reaching it. But if the resources to reach it are available, people can be blamed for their failure.

If that sounds too complicated, think of a rusty nut on a bicycle. No-one could be blamed for failing to undo it with his or her fingernails. But if a can of penetrating oil and a power-assisted socket set is available, the person who insists on using his or her own fingers can rightly be held responsible for failing to do the job.

(iii) *Deciding by results.* Of the three main routes to making moral decisions, the third one (deciding by results) is certainly the most popular. Unfortunately, it is also the least reliable. The person who takes this route may decide that breaking a trad-itional standard cannot be wrong because he or she sees no harm in the consequences. But disaster may meet him or her unex-pectedly around the third or fourth bend of the road.

The trouble is that forecasting results of behaviour is a much more uncertain business than telling what the weather is going to do next week! I can usually decide fairly accurately whether a word or an action of mine is likely to cause harm in five minutes' time — or even next week, or next month. But the further I look into the future, the less reliable my forecasting will be. Some actions which bring short-term good results can have very bad long-term effects.

Christians believe that keeping God's standards protects them from making long-term mistakes. They may not see, for example, how failing to keep the strict 'no sex before marriage' standard can possibly do anyone any harm, but they keep it just the same, in the confidence that God's long-range forecasting is more reli-able than their own. Jesus made this point very simply in his parable of the two builders (see *Matthew* 7:24–27). The man who took a short cut by ignoring building standards ended up as the long-term loser. Exactly the same would happen, warned Jesus, to 'anyone who hears these words of mine and does not obey them.'

## Questions for discussion

1. Do you think moral standards have slipped? If so, is this necessarily a bad thing?
2. Why have people's attitudes towards traditional standards changed?
3. 'It can't be wrong if there's no harm in it.' Do you agree?

# 2. Love and rules

In the last chapter, I suggested that when people talk about standards, they usually mean moral *rules*. That is certainly the way many people think about Christian standards. Christians, they assume, are those who obey the Ten Commandments and live by the rules which Jesus laid out in the Sermon on the Mount.

When we look more closely at the New Testament, however, we find that Jesus did not agree at all with a 'rule-book only' approach to moral living. The champion rule-keepers of his time were the Scribes and Pharisees, and he often criticized them very sharply for the standards they taught and encouraged.

**The limits of rule-keeping**

The most startling criticism Jesus made was that living by rules sets moral standards too low. 'I tell you', he warned his disciples, 'that unless your righteousness *surpasses* that of the Pharisees and the teachers of the law, you will certainly not enter the kingdom of heaven.' (*Matthew* 5:20).

In his frequent clashes with the Scribes and Pharisees, Jesus made it quite clear what he meant. For one thing, he said, making all decisions by the rule-book can actually lead people to *evade their responsibilities*. In the parable of the Good Samaritan, the priest who hurried past the bleeding man in the gutter was obeying the small print of his rule-book. He was afraid that the wounded man was already dead. The law said that anyone who touched a corpse was ritually unclean for seven days (see *Numbers* 19:11). The priest was not prepared to risk losing his turn of duty in the Temple, so he turned a blind eye to the man's need. It was the despised Samaritan who stopped to help, because he was not tied in the same way by the red tape of the Jewish law.

There were even times, Jesus pointed out, when people who actually wanted to *escape* their responsibilities found a valuable ally in the rule-book. The Ten Commandments said very clearly that children must respect their parents. That was taken to mean that a grown-up son should support his father and mother financially in their old age. It was a first-class principle, especially in times when there were no pension schemes, but some unscrupulous sons had found a neat, legal way of side-stepping it. There was a by-law which said that any money dedicated to God must not be touched by anyone else. It was a simple matter, therefore, to declare your money 'Corban' (dedicated to God), and then say to your elderly parents, 'I'm sorry, but I've nothing left to give you'.

Jesus' comment on that use of the rule-book was biting: 'In this way the teaching you pass on to others cancels out the word of God. And there are many other things like this that you do.' (*Mark* 7:9–13).

Even when the rule-book was not used as an escape-route, its mass of detail could *hide important principles*. Jesus drew attention to this also, especially in his clashes with the Pharisees over observing the sabbath.

Long before Jesus' day, the Jewish lawyers had found that the simple commandment, 'Observe the Sabbath and keep it holy' had far too many loop-holes in it. So they tried to define exactly what sabbath observance meant, and in particular what kinds of work were forbidden on the seventh day. The result was a vast network of trivial by-laws, in 39 separate sections. There was a rule which told you what to do if you cut your finger on the sabbath day, another which limited the help you could give your wife if she was unlucky enough to have a baby on the sabbath, and another that set out instructions for action you could take if a wall fell on top of your neighbour.

Somewhere, underneath this heap of detail, was buried the main principle the sabbath was meant to protect. 'The Sabbath was made for the good of man', said Jesus; 'man was not made for the Sabbath' (*Mark* 2:27). The whole point of the sabbath was to make sure that working people had a day off, but the rule-book had turned a holiday camp into a prison. And the law-men had become the jailers, making sure that everyone stayed locked in his or her cell.

**Character and motives**

Jesus' main quarrel with the rule-keepers was that they set their standards too low. So what alternative did he have to suggest?

A conversation with Peter pointed the way. Peter asked him, 'Lord, if my brother keeps on sinning against me, how many times do I have to forgive him? Seven times?' Jesus replied, 'No, not seven times, but seventy times seven.' (*Matthew* 18:21–22).

Peter had asked a rule-keeping kind of question. He wanted a regulation which would set a limit on his duty to forgive. Jesus refused to give him one. By 'seventy times seven', he did not mean Peter to count up to 490! What he required of Peter was a forgiving *spirit*, an *attitude of mind* which forgave without counting.

This was the level at which Jesus set his standards. And he made no secret of the fact that standards like these were far more demanding than keeping rules. He illustrated their challenge very vividly in the Sermon on the Mount by referring to sins of sex and violence. The rule-book said 'Do not commit adultery' and 'Do not commit murder.' But Jesus probed more deeply than that. A man might keep on the right side of the rules by never committing adultery, but what about the thoughts that go through his mind when he sees his neighbour's wife passing by his bedroom window? 'Anyone who looks at a woman and wants to possess her is guilty of committing adultery with her *in his heart*', said Jesus. He may never attack her husband physically, let alone murder him, but what about the hostile thoughts that pass through his mind? They will never put him in the dock on a murder charge, but 'anyone who is angry with his brother without cause', said Jesus, 'will be subject to judgement' (*Matthew* 5:21–22, 27–28).

Jesus taught that a person's thought-life is as important as his or her conduct. After all, our actions spring from those inner attitudes of the mind and heart which motivate us (see *Matthew* 12:33–35). And the very best actions turn sour when they are badly motivated. Giving to charity, for instance, is obviously a good thing to do, but it is thoroughly spoiled if donors give for selfish reasons, because they want everyone to admire their generosity (see *Matthew* 6:1–4). God is not only interested in outward behaviour; he inspects the heart (see *1 Samuel* 16:7).

So the main question Jesus asked, as far as moral standards were concerned, was not 'Are you keeping all the rules?', but

'What kind of a person are you becoming?'. He was certainly concerned about conduct (see, for example, *Matthew* 7:16–21), but he was far more concerned about character. The so-called Beatitudes, which begin the Sermon on the Mount, have been nicknamed 'the Beautiful Attitudes' because they focus far more on character than on behaviour. They are not a list of rules at all, but a set of congratulations from God to those whose standards are high because their attitudes are right (see *Matthew* 5:1–12).

## Love

When Jesus was asked which of the Old Testament's laws was the most important, it came as no surprise when he picked out two commands which dealt with inward attitudes. 'The most important one', he replied, 'is this: "Hear, O Israel, the Lord our God, the Lord is one. Love the Lord your God with all your heart and with all your soul and with all your mind and with all you strength." The second is this: "Love your neighbour as yourself." There is no commandment greater than these.' (*Mark* 12:28–31; see *Deuteronomy* 6:4–5 and *Leviticus* 19:18).

Love is the ultimate standard the New Testament applies in judging all conduct. Without it, writes Paul in a famous passage, the best actions (including gifts to charity and even martyrdom) are worthless (see *1 Corinthians* 13:1–3).

It is vital, however, to pin down exactly what the New Testament means by 'love', because the word can be used with so many different shades of meaning today. Depending on circumstances, we can use it to mean almost anything from having sexual intercourse ('making love') to treating a pet kindly ('loving your dog') or enjoying the food and the scenery ('I love strawberries — and those hills').

In the Greek world of New Testament times, there were several different words for 'love'. One was *eros*, the love of physical attraction. Another was *philia*, the love of friendship. And a third was *storgē* (pronounced stor-gay), the love of family affection. But when the New Testament writers wanted to describe what Jesus meant by 'love', they found all the usual words inadequate. So they hit upon another, one that had hardly been used before, the word *agapē* (pronounced aga-pay).

*Agapē* love, as Jesus lived and taught it, was unique. First, it was different from *eros*, because it meant loving the unattractive. You could not have *eros* for someone who did not attract you, but *agapē* embraced those you found least lovable. Secondly, it was different from *philia*, because it meant loving the unresponsive. 'You have heard that it was said, "love your friends, hate your enemies." But now I tell you' (said Jesus), 'love your enemies.' (*Matthew* 5:43–45). You could not have *philia* for someone who did not return your friendship, but *agapē* loved on even when it got no love back (see *Luke* 6:32–35). And thirdly, *agapē* was different from *storgē* because it meant loving the stranger. You could only have *storgē* for those inside the family circle, but *agapē* reached out to include anyone in need, whether you knew the person or not (see *Luke* 10:25–37).

This was the kind of love that Jesus illustrated by the way he lived, and the love he commanded his followers to copy (see *John* 15:12). So when Christians talk about 'standards', they mean above everything else the *agapē* standard that Jesus set.

**Love and rules**

Did Jesus, then, have no time for rule-keeping at all? When he summed up the whole Old Testament law in the command to love, was he really saying, 'You can throw all your rule books out of the window. Provided you love, you can do what you like.'?

There is plenty of evidence that Jesus did not mean that at all. He respected and reinforced the Old Testament's moral law himself. 'Whoever disobeys even the least important of the commandments and teaches others to do the same', he told his disciples, 'will be least in the kingdom of heaven.' (*Matthew* 5:17–19). What is more, he laid down some very clear main-line rules of his own and obviously expected his followers to keep them (see *Matthew* 7:24).

Rules certainly have their uses. For one thing, *they provide us with moral information*. Love cannot tell us the difference between right and wrong on its own. If you put half a dozen people in the same situation and say, 'Now do the loving thing', they are quite likely to do half a dozen different things. As one modern writer puts it, 'Law is love's eyes, and without law to give it vision, love is blind.' The Bible says the same thing in different words: 'what the Law does is to make man know that he has sinned.' (*Romans* 3:20).

Then again, *rules stimulate our consciences*. They remind us forcibly of important moral standards which we might otherwise

*Rules must be kept! Or can we challenge them? Here the referee's decision was contested. People today often disagree with decisions made by those in authority. Some even argue that if an Act of Parliament is, in their view, 'bad law' they are justified in disobeying it. How do you feel about such attitudes? And where could they lead?*

forget or ignore. The conscience stops pricking when a person disobeys it often enough (see *1 Timothy* 4:2). The reminder of a rule can bring it to life again.

There is an important sense, too, in which *rules protect our freedom*. Just as the rules of football make the game flow more freely, so a good law does not shrink people's liberty, but enlarges it. The laws against assault, for example, mean that we are free to walk the streets more safely. Jesus himself linked obedience with freedom when he said, 'If you obey my teaching, you are really my disciples; you will know the truth, and the truth will set you free.' (*John* 8:31–32).

The New Testament's formula is not love *or* rules, but love *and* rules. It aims to set out God's rules for living alongside the significance of God's love for daily life. They are not two different standards which clash. They belong together like two sides of the same coin (see *John* 15:10 and *1 John* 5:3). Love gives rule-keeping its warmth and sensitivity, and rules give love their firmness and direction.

### Questions for discussion

1. What are the disadvantages in sticking rigidly to a rule-book?
2. What problem did the Jewish treatment of the sabbath law illustrate? Can you think of any modern parallels?
3. Do you agree with Jesus' view that people's inward attitudes are as important as their outward conduct?
4. How do your ideas about love compare with Jesus' teaching?

*Part B*

# Personal relationships

## 3. Family life

What is a family? You probably live in one, so you think you know. But family life can take many different forms. Most children live with their mother and father, and at least one brother or sister, but there are all sorts of other family patterns too. There are 'only' children, children living with just one parent (usually the mother), and children with different fathers or mothers living under the same roof after a divorce. There are also, of course, many children who live without either parent. Their home life is just as important as anyone else's.

Ask some people how big their families are, and they will give you a list with no more than four or five names on it — mum, dad, brother, sister (the so-called 'nuclear' family). Ask others, and it seems as though the list could go on for ever — grandmas, grandads, cousins, uncles, great-aunts, and all sorts of adult friends who may be known as 'uncle' and 'auntie', because they are treated as part of the so-called 'extended' family.

Nor must we forget that there are many homes without children. There are married couples in their thirties who go out to work and have never wanted babies. There are couples who *cannot* have children. And there are others in their fifties and sixties whose children have grown up and left home. We must come back to them and their needs before the end of this chapter.

The family pattern has certainly changed a great deal in the last 50 years. Some of the changes have made family life better. On the whole, for example, the nuclear family is smaller, which means that many children get more personal attention than they used to. However badly off we may think we are, there is also more money around today to buy things for our homes. And rising health standards mean that modern families have to face death far less often than our great-grandparents did in Victorian times.

It would be stupid, however, to pretend that those T.V. advertisements for breakfast cereals reflect modern family life in *every* home. Does every family have a handsome, successful father, plus a good-looking, home-loving mother and two bright, adorable children sitting round the breakfast table with happy smiles at 8 o'clock in the morning? If we are honest, we have to admit that for many people today family life is more like hell than heaven. And some of the changes society has brought upon us do not help.

Many more marriages end in divorce now than ever before, and no child can remain unaffected when his or her parents separate. More mothers go out to work than ever before — but, if the fathers are out at work too, it can be very lonely, if you are a child, to get back from school to an empty home and find your own tea. More elderly members of families live further away than ever before, and that can lead to great loneliness, too. Not all the changes have been for the better.

Some alternatives to the pattern of nuclear family life have been suggested and tried. One of the most interesting modern experiments is the Israeli *kibbutz*, where the community owns all the property and brings up the children. In the early days of the *kibbutz* scheme, nuclear family relationships were frowned upon. Now, however, there are signs of change. Israeli children are encouraged to call their natural parents 'father' and 'mother'. Family housekeeping is coming back, too, with meals taken together in family flats. So even in the *kibbutz* the nuclear family is regaining its popularity. It seems as though family life (of the mother, father and children kind) is a need written so deeply into the heart of human nature that it cannot be ignored.

**God and the family**

This comes as no surprise to Christians, because the idea of the family is at the heart of the Christian gospel. Jesus encouraged his disciples, when they talked to God, not to pray to an Almighty Deity but to say 'Our Father' (see *Matthew* 6:9). And he often used the human family as a model to teach vital truths. The greatness of God's forgiveness, for example, comes across with amazing clarity in the parable of the lost son (see *Luke* 15:11–32).

The rest of the New Testament echoes Jesus' use of family

language. 'Those who are led by God's Spirit are God's sons', writes Paul to the Christians at Rome. 'The Spirit makes you God's children', he goes on, 'and by the Spirit's power we cry out to God, "Father! my Father!" ' (*Romans* 8:14–15). In another letter he describes God as 'the Father, from whom every family, whether spiritual or natural, takes its name' (*Ephesians* 3:14–15). There we have an echo of the first chapter of the Bible, where God reveals himself as a kind of family, and deliberately makes human beings to be like him (see *Genesis* 1:26–27).

In case this 'father talk' sounds too masculine for the age of Women's Liberation, it is interesting to see that the Bible sometimes describes God as a mother. 'You will be like a child that is nursed by its mother, carried in her arms and treated with love', the Lord tells his people. 'I will comfort you in Jerusalem as a mother comforts her child.' (*Isaiah* 66:12–13).

**Parents and children**

The Bible also has some quite detailed guidance about the way parents and children should relate to each other in the home. Some of this teaching sounds odd, because patterns of family life have altered drastically since biblical times, but under the details are important principles which are as valid now as they were then.

You may find it disappointing to see no signs of 'children's liberation' in the New Testament! Paul is quite clear that young children should do exactly what they are told: 'Children, it is your Christian duty to obey your parents always, for that is what pleases God.' (*Colossians* 3:20; see also *Ephesians* 6:1). If his readers had any doubts at all about that, they only had to remember the example Jesus himself set as a boy. 'He went down to Nazareth with them (Joseph and Mary) and was obedient to them.' (*Luke* 2:51).

Paul is very careful, though, to balance this demand for obedience with some clear instructions to parents. 'Parents, do not irritate your children', he warns, 'or they will become discouraged.' (*Colossians* 3:21). His word for 'irritate' was also used for challenging someone to a boxing match. The father who picks quarrels with his children, demanding their obedience 'or else', is just being a bully. That kind of so-called 'discipline' only creates tension in the home. Martin Luther, the great German church leader, had a father like that. Relationships at home were so bad that as a boy he found it impossible to say the beginning of the Lord's Prayer. 'Spare the rod and spoil the child, it is true', he wrote later, 'but beside the rod keep an apple to give him when he does well.'

The Old Testament insists that a good thump is not necessarily unloving. 'Children just naturally do silly, careless things, but a good spanking will teach them how to behave', says the Book of Proverbs cheerfully. 'If you don't punish your son, you don't love him. If you do love him, you will correct him.' (*Proverbs* 22:15, 13:24). We may disagree with the detail of corporal punishment (or do we?), but the principle of discipline remains. The New Testament, as well as the Old, teaches that parents who love their children will discipline them (see, for example *Hebrews* 12:5–11).

One aspect of bringing up children that the Bible stresses very strongly is moral training. 'Pay attention to what you father and mother tell you, my son. Their teaching will improve your character.' (*Proverbs* 1:8–9). In Old Testament times, God's commandments were even written on door-posts, so that no member of the family would grow up without knowing the difference between right and wrong (see *Deuteronomy* 6:4–9). In some Jewish families that is still done today.

What happens, though, when a child *does* grow up? Does the relationship between child and parent change, once a son or daughter becomes independent?

The Bible has plenty to say about this as well. Jesus set the pattern himself, both in his teaching and by his example. As we have seen, he obeyed Joseph and Mary when he was a boy (though there was a misunderstanding about his 'father', when he got lost on the way home from Jerusalem — see *Luke* 2:41–52). Once he was a grown man, however, there were times when he went completely against his mother's wishes (see, for example, *Matthew* 12:46–50). He also taught his disciples that there are at least three turning-points in a grown-up child's life when parents must take second place — getting married (see *Matthew* 19:4–5), discovering and following a vocation (see *Luke* 18:28–29), and making a personal commitment of faith (see *Luke* 9:57–62). These are three things that parents cannot decide for their children.

Two Bible words mark the difference between childhood and adulthood, as far as Christian family relationships are concerned. Paul uses them both in his letter to the Ephesians: 'Children *obey*

When 'home' is just a cardboard box on a dirty pavement, 'family life' is little more than a helping hand from a stranger. Does this mean that any home is better than none? Is cutting yourself off from the company of others the worst thing you can do?

your parents . . . *Honour* your father and mother . . .' (*Ephesians* 6:1–2). 'Obeying' stops when a child becomes an adult, but 'honouring' goes on and means more.

The Bible word for 'honour' actually means 'treat as weighty' or 'regard as important'. Again, Jesus himself brought the meaning of that word to life by his personal example. As a grown man he may not always have done exactly what his mother wanted, but he never stopped treating her as important. Even while he was dying in agony on the cross, she was important enough for him to find time and breath to provide for her needs (see *John* 19:26).

The trouble comes, of course, in adolescence — that in-between time when the demands to obey have not stopped, and the duty of honouring does not come at all easily. *You* think you are an adult, but *your parents* still treat you as a child. Family relationships can be stretched to breaking point when you are told in your last term at school what to wear for a party and what time to get home afterwards!

Parents can try to keep their position of authority too long, but children can claim their independence too soon. Jesus' story of the lost son showed in an unforgettable way how being determined to become independent too quickly can lead to disaster. Perhaps the best biblical test, from the teenager's angle, is to ask yourself whether you honestly attach great weight to your parents' opinions and wishes, even when you disagree with them. If the answer is 'no' or 'not sure', you have probably not outgrown the obedience stage.

**The extended family**

Parents of young children are at the very centre of the nuclear family. But when their sons and daughters grow up and make them grandparents, they are often pushed out of the family circle altogether.

In Britain today, apart from some ethnic minority groups in our larger towns and cities, the idea of the extended family has almost died. As Ronald Fletcher, a social scientist, puts it: 'The extended family — the large independent network of extended kindred — is outmoded in a modern industrial society. The days of the clan and of the village network of aunts, uncles and forty-second cousins are over.'

This change is not a good one. It is especially serious because there are many more elderly people around than ever before. State care for old people is no substitute for the warmth of family support. A recent survey predicted a rise of 20 per cent in the number of people over 75 between now and the year 2000. It also included figures to show that 34 per cent of all people over 65 now live alone. Alone-ness is not the same as loneliness, of course, but for many elderly people the one leads to the other.

In biblical times, the idea of the extended family was very much alive. Even your forty-second cousin was 'bone of your bone and flesh of your flesh' (see, for example, *Judges* 9:2 and 2 *Samuel* 5:1). The elderly were treated with enormous respect (see *Proverbs* 23:22). Although the structures of our society are so different, modern Christians have plenty to learn from the Bible's insistence that the young and healthy have a responsibility for the weak and elderly. Jesus himself spoke out strongly against those who made excuses to avoid helping their ageing parents (see *Mark* 7:9–13). And Paul's words to Timothy were even stronger: 'If anyone does not take care of his relatives, especially the members of his own family, he has denied the faith and is worse than an unbeliever.' (1 *Timothy* 5:8).

**Questions for discussion**

1. How do you see the future of family life?
2. How serious an effect does a broken marriage have on the future life of children?
3. Is the Bible's idea of firm but fair discipline what children need?
4. How much responsibility do we have towards weak and elderly members of the family? Could more be done to help them?

# 4. Sex and sexism

Why are men and women different? The answer seems obvious, but there are in fact several different ways you can reply to that kind of question.

At the *physical* level, our sex is fixed at birth for most of us. A tiny minority of people are born with their sexual identity undecided.Their special needs must not be ignored, but in the vast majority of cases the midwife can tell the mother, 'It's a boy' or 'It's a girl' as soon as her baby appears. Our sexual characteristics develop as the years go by, but without a sex-change operation we can do nothing about the fact that we are either male or female from the moment we are born.

At the *emotional* level, however, the differences become a little blurred. We all have some of the three main sex hormones in our bodies — androgen, oestrogen and progesterone — but the exact balance differs from person to person. The 'mix' will affect our feelings as well as our shape and looks. Most men are aggressive — as well as being more muscular. Most women are tender — as well as having more fatty tissue. But it is impossible to generalize. There are tender men and aggressive women. This makes it very important that we do not pay too much attention to the male and female stereotypes we find in the glossy magazines.

At the *social* level, the differences between boys and girls are sharpened from a very early age. Many baby-clothes are either blue or pink. Children are given different toys — small boys get guns, small girls get dolls. And though there has been some change in schools' policy, the feeling is still strong in society as a whole that boys should prepare themselves for a life-time career, while girls look beyond their first job to finding 'Mr Right' and starting a family.

**Sexism**

If there are any feminists in the class, their blood may be boiling by now! The problem, as the feminist sees it, is that society has turned these sexual distinctions we have listed into grounds for making women inferior to men. Men are not just different; they are superior. That, at any rate, is what the pressures of our society and culture persuade us to believe. In a male-dominated world, women's place is to respond to men's desires and demands.

'Sexism' is the word used to describe all attitudes and actions which subordinate one person to another on grounds of sex. And feminists identify two main areas of life where this kind of discrimination still rules.

In the first place, there is the way *women are treated as sex-objects*, instead of as people. One American writer tells about a girl she knew who complained, 'When I turned out to be a mathematical genius, my mother said, "Put on some lip-stick and see if you can find a boyfriend." '

You do not have to be good at maths to feel that kind of pressure if you are a girl! A well-known woman's magazine asked its readers, 'How often do you spend an evening making yourself truly feminine like plucking your eyebrows, toning your skin, giving yourself a pedicure, etc.?' The same article then goes on to explain, 'The natural ambition of every woman is to be happy and to keep her husband content. What you have to understand is that men need to be kept aware of their possessions and, unfortunately, you come into that category.'

Secondly, there is the way *women are treated as mentally and psychologically inferior*. Men *think*, it is said, while women only *feel*. Women act impulsively, while men reason things out before acting. Men are both intelligent and straightforward; women are either stupid or cunning.

That kind of biased sexist outlook is summed up very well in two ancient proverbs from different parts of the world. 'The glory of a man is knowledge', say the Chinese, 'but the glory of a woman is to renounce knowledge.' 'Whenever a woman dies', add the Germans, 'there is one less quarrel on earth.'

**The church and sexism**

The Christian church has not had a very good record as far as sexism is concerned. At the end of the second century, for example, Bishop Tertullian of North Africa openly blamed woman for man's fall into sin. 'Do you not know', he asked his lady readers, 'that each of you is also an Eve? You are the devil's gateway, you are the first deserter of the divine law, you were the one who persuaded him whom the devil was too weak to attack.'

In the Middle Ages, the great theologian Thomas Aquinas taught that men should always be the leaders because only in the male sex does 'the discretion of reason predominate'. Three hundred years later, John Knox, the Scottish Reformer, published a tract called *The First Blast of the Trumpet against the Monstrous Regiment of Women*. It began, 'To promote a woman to bear rule is repugnant to nature; contumely to God, a thing most contrarious to his revealed will and approved ordinance; and finally it is subversive of good order, of all equity and justice.'

Knox aimed this attack at Queen Mary. He would doubtless have been equally angry at the idea of a woman becoming Prime Minister nowadays. And his fellow-Reformer in Germany, Martin Luther, would have found a lady head-of-state equally hard to accept. 'Men have broad and large chests', wrote Luther, 'and small narrow hips, and more understanding than women, who have but small and narrow chests, and broad hips, to the end that they should remain at home, sit still, keep house, and bear and bring up children.'

With statements like these from its leaders, it is no wonder that the church is the arch-enemy of women, in many feminists' eyes. After all, isn't the Christian idea of God *him*self sexist? Why should he be 'King' rather than 'Queen'? Why shouldn't we pray 'Our Mother' instead of 'Our Father'?

**The Bible and sexism**

The Church may have earned these criticisms, but it has done so only because it has departed from the teaching and example of Jesus. And while the Bible agrees that sexism exists, it traces it to man's rebellion against God, not to God's will for mankind.

God is certainly always 'he' in the Bible, but that is only to distinguish him as a person. 'He' is not an 'it'. Occasionally, the

*Who says that some jobs are for men only? Eighteen-year-old Antonette Shaw proves that women can drive buses too. But should women have to prove themselves in this way? Will they ever really have 'equal opportunities'?*

Bible actually describes God in female picture-language. Isaiah, for example, compares him to a woman in childbirth (*Isaiah* 42:14) and a nursing mother (*Isaiah* 49:15, 66:13).

God is beyond all sexual distinctions, as Jesus made clear when he taught, 'God is *spirit*, and those who worship *him* must worship in spirit and in truth.' (*John* 4:24). That is one reason why, in Old Testament times, God's people were told not to make an image of him, 'whether formed like a man or a woman'. (*Deuteronomy* 4:15–18).

Jesus, too, though a man, had characteristics which we might label today as more feminine than masculine. He was strong, resolute and decisive. But he did not consider it unmanly to be tender, gentle and loving as well; or to cry in public (see, for example, *John* 11:35 and *Luke* 13:34, 19:41).

By his personal example, Jesus also made it very clear that he did not discriminate between people in a sexist way. He taught in the temple's Court of Women, showing that in his view women were every bit as intelligent and teachable as men. He startled a Samaritan woman by getting into conversation with her by a well (see *John* 4:4–9). And he included some women among his disciples (see *Luke* 8:1–3).

This may not sound at all remarkable to us, but in Jesus' day it was revolutionary. He lived in a strongly sexist society. An orthodox Jewish male of Jesus' time was meant to thank God daily in his prayers that he had not been made a gentile, a slave — or a woman.

How did it come about that God's people had slipped so far into sexist attitudes, when God Himself was against sexism? For an answer, the Bible takes us back to God's creation scheme and man's rebellion against it.

The creation story of Genesis leaves no room at all for sexist discrimination. 'When God created human beings, he made them like himself. He created them male and female, blessed them, and named them "Mankind".' (Genesis 5:1–2). From the moment of creation, according to the Bible, man and woman were made absolutely equal. Moreover, God gave to both sexes *together* the responsibilities of home-making and creative work (see *Genesis* 1:28). The modern division between having a satisfying career (men's department) and looking after the children (women's department), with all its sexist implications, was not there at the beginning in the Creator's plan.

According to Genesis, division and conflict between the sexes arose directly from their rebellion against God. One of the most interesting comments that the book of Genesis makes about the impact of sin on human relationships concerns nudity. Before their fall into sin, 'the man and his wife were both naked, and they felt no shame'. Afterwards, 'the eyes of both of them were opened, and they realized they were naked.' (*Genesis* 2:25 and 3:7). From that time on, they saw each other in a new way. When man looked at woman, he now saw a sex-object first, not a person. And from that moment, according to the Bible, conflict between the sexes was born. 'Your desire will be for your husband', God predicted to woman, 'and he will rule over you.' (*Genesis* 3:16).

As we have seen, Jesus came to put an end to all discrimination and conflict. Both in his teaching and by his example, he smashed the barriers his society had erected between the sexes. And the first Christians fought hard against sexist trends as they carried his gospel to different places. Paul, for example, bracketed together sexism, racism and class discrimination as three kinds of broken human relationships which Jesus came to mend. 'There is no difference', he wrote, 'between Jews and Gentiles, between slaves and free men, between men and women; you are all one in union with Christ Jesus.' (*Galatians* 3:28).

Equality, however, is not sameness. Paul meant that men and women were equal in status, not identical in role and function. Here the Bible does clash with the more extreme feminists who complain that men have made child-bearing into a weapon to oppress women.

Christian teaching has a much higher view of marriage and motherhood than that. Historically it has, perhaps, underplayed the Bible's teaching on the duties of fatherhood. Nevertheless, Christians resist the suggestion that women who stay at home and look after the children are doing something second-rate. The fact that a mother is physically equipped to feed her baby does not make her inferior, but it does make her different.

## Questions for discussion

1. Are the Bible's views on sexism radical enough?
2. What more should be done to stamp out stereotyped sexist ideas?
3. How do the roles of men and women vary in different countries and communities?

# 5. Friendship, love and marriage

In the last chapter we considered the gap that separates the Church's traditional attitude to sex *discrimination* from the Bible's strongly positive teaching on equality. Now, as we move on to consider friendship and marriage, we find a very similar split between biblical and traditional church attitudes towards sexual *feelings*.

This may seem puzzling. After all, the Bible is the church's guide-book, so why the division? The answer is that at a very early date Greek philosophy and oriental religion influenced the church very strongly indeed. Among other things, teachers who were soaked in these traditions taught that the life of the body was inferior to the life of the soul. It followed, they said, that sexual desire, as a physical thing, should be swept under the carpet where (in their minds) it belonged with the rest of the dirt.

It is easy to find illustrations of this anti-sex trend in the pages of early church history. Many early Christian writers seized on the fact that Jesus and John the Baptist never married, and used this to prove that saying a loud 'no' to sex is pleasing to God. Ambrose, bishop of Milan in the fourth century, once said, 'Married people ought to blush when they consider the sort of life they live.' Another early Christian writer, the author of *The Acts of John*, described sexual intercourse as 'an experiment of the serpent . . . the impediment that separates from the Lord.'

Not all church leaders were as negative as that, but until the time of the European Reformation in the sixteenth century it was generally assumed that Christians who wanted to live their lives at the highest spiritual level should avoid all sexual contact. The clergy, in particular, were expected to remain virgins for life, (and in thirteenth-century England about one in 12 men was a clergyman).

## The Bible and sex

The Bible's attitude to sex is far more positive. The story of creation sets the scene. God's first command to man and woman involved sexual intercourse (see *Genesis* 1:28). He deliberately made them as sexual beings, and when he had finished his work of creation he pronounced everything — including sex — 'very good' (*Genesis* 1:31).

In sharp contrast to Greek and oriental views, the Bible puts a very high value on the body. The climax came, of course, in the incarnation of Jesus (see *John* 1:14). It was 'in his body', writes Peter, that Christ 'carried our sins' (*1 Peter* 2:24). And Christians must respond by using their bodies for God's glory, says Paul (see *1 Corinthians* 6:20).

So, far from playing down physical attractiveness, the Bible delights in it. Listen, for example, to the way *The Song of Solomon* describes the two-way feelings of a genuine love-match:

*The man:*     'Your eyes are doves behind your veil . . . Your lips are like a scarlet thread and your mouth is lovely . . . You are all fair, my love; there is no fault in you . . . You have ravished my heart with a glance of your eyes.'

*The woman:* 'My lover is handsome and strong . . . I belong to my lover, and he desires me . . . My lover is mine, and I am his . . . I am sick with love!'

In the light of this very positive outlook, it comes as no surprise to find that the Bible is not at all embarrassed about physical gestures of friendship. Jesus himself allowed a prostitute to show her affection for him physically (*Luke* 7:38), and the Old Testament describes David and Jonathan's friendship in a way that leaves some modern readers embarrassed: 'David got up from behind a pile of stones, fell on his knees and bowed with his face to the ground three times. Both he and Jonathan were crying as they kissed each other.' (*1 Samuel* 20:41). David was far from being a homosexual (see, for example, *2 Samuel* 11:2–5), but when Jonathan died he expressed his grief in a very intimate way: 'I grieve for you, my brother Jonathan; how dear you were to me! How wonderful was your love for me, better even than the love of women.' (*2 Samuel* 1:26).

**Sexual intercourse**

What, then, about the climax of physical intimacy, sexual intercourse? On this, the Bible seems to speak with two voices.

Both the Old Testament and the New are openly enthusiastic
about the enjoyment a *married couple* ought to find in sexual
intercourse. 'Rejoice in the wife of your youth', the Old Testament tells a young husband, 'Let her affection fill you at all times
with delight, be infatuated always with her love.' (*Proverbs* 5:18–
19). And in the New Testament Paul strikes the same note,
though in a more subdued way, when he writes to Christian
couples worried by heretical anti-sex teaching: 'A wife is not the
master of her own body, but her husband is; in the same way a
husband is not the master of his own body, but his wife is. Do
not deny yourselves to each other.' (*1 Corinthians* 7:4–5).

To the *unmarried*, on the other hand, the Bible bans sexual
intercourse altogether. Jesus included all intercourse outside marriage in a list of those things which 'make a person unclean' (see
*Mark* 7:20–23). Paul, too, listed extra-marital sex among those
things which are out of character for those who belong to the
Kingdom of God (see *1 Corinthians* 6:9–11). 'God wants you to be
holy and completely free from sexual immorality', he wrote in
another of his letters (*1 Thessalonians* 4:3).

This ban sounds ridiculous to many modern people. 'You've
got to grab sex while you can, I reckon', said one 17-year-old to
a newspaper reporter. 'I mean, it's sheer hypocrisy for the older
generation to prevent teenagers from doing something so *natural*
and *amazing*.' She had been on the pill since she was 14. Perhaps
she would have thought differently if she had lived before the
pill had been invented. As it was, medicine had given her all she
wanted to avoid getting pregnant, and all she needed to get over
V.D. if she was unlucky enough to catch it.

So where is the harm in having sex before marriage? The Bible
does not answer by talking about disease and unwanted babies.
It reaches back much further for a reason — back, in fact, to the
whole purpose of sexual intercourse in human life.

*From the negative angle*, the New Testament insists that sex is
not just a physical appetite. If it were, Alex Comfort (the psy-
chologist) would have been quite right when he claimed that
'chastity is no more a virtue than malnutrition'. Why force yourself to starve if you have a good appetite when plenty of food is
available?

Paul criticized this 'appetite only' view of sex in his first letter to the church at Corinth. Some of these Christians thought about having sex in much the same way as they thought about having a good meal. After all, they said, 'Food is for the stomach, and the stomach is for food'. 'Yes', replied Paul, 'but the body is not to be used for sexual immorality.' He talks about prostitution to make his point clear. 'Do you not know that if a man joins himself to a prostitute she becomes a part of him and he becomes a part of her? For God tells us in the Scriptures that in his sight the two become one person.' (*1 Corinthians* 6:12–20)

In other words, having sex is not like famine relief. There is no such thing as 'casual' intercourse. Sexual intercourse affects us as whole persons, not just as bundles of appetites. Those who look at sex as a monkey looks at a banana have got it all wrong, according to the Bible, because they have made sex too small.

*From the positive angle*, the Bible teaches that the purpose of sexual intercourse is to cement a relationship of a special kind. The story of creation in Genesis stresses the point that God made sexuality in the first place to fill a relationship gap in human life. And man's reaction when woman was brought to him underlines the special character of that relationship. 'This at last', he said 'is bone of my bone and flesh of my flesh.' (see *Genesis* 2:18–23)

Sex is for relationship. This is the message that rings out loud and clear throughout the Bible. And sexual intercourse is body-language of a special kind. A touch and a kiss are ways in which a friend can say 'I like you a lot'. Intercourse means far more than that. It says, 'I intend to give myself to you for life.' That is the main reason why Christian teaching is against having sex before marriage. Those who think otherwise are (in Christianity's view) wrong, because they are making intercourse mean less than it should.

The Bible lays down no rules for 'how far you should go' before marriage, but it does warn its readers about the enormous power of the average person's sex drive once it gets out of control. Paul was very realistic about this. 'Run away' was the advice he gave to one young person he knew (see *2 Timothy* 2:22). Perhaps he had in the back of his mind the Old Testament story of Joseph and Potiphar's wife. 'She caught Joseph by his garment, saying "Come to bed with me". But he left his garment in her hand, and fled.' (*Genesis* 39:12)

**Marriage and singleness**

Christianity sets a very high value on marriage, but it is careful to define exactly what marriage means. This is important, because a marriage is not the same as a wedding. Wedding ceremonies vary from place to place and from time to time, but the essential principles of marriage remain the same.

The Bible lists three such principles. They are first put together in the book of Genesis, and in the New Testament both Jesus and Paul take them up and emphasize their importance in a fresh way. (see *Genesis* 2:24, *Mark* 10:7–8 and *Ephesians* 5:31)

*First*, there is *the involvement of society*. Genesis puts this in the simplest possible way: 'a man leaves his father and mother'. In biblical times, leaving home was an elaborate affair. The ceremony took days, and involved everyone in the community. Today, in Britain, the whole thing can be done in front of two witnesses in ten minutes. Either way, the principle remains the same. Marriage is not a completely private affair between two people in love. It involves the breaking up of a vital social unit (parent and child) and the making of a new one (husband and wife). These are the bricks from which the whole structure of society, ancient or modern, is built.

*Secondly*, the couple must declare their *lifelong loyalty and trust to each other*: 'a man is united with his wife'. The Bible word for 'unite' also means 'stick'. In other words, those who marry must intend to stand by one another for life. Each will give himself or herself completely to the other. This is what love in marriage is all about, writes Paul (see *Ephesians* 5:24–25). Husbands and wives only fall out of love when they stop giving, not when they stop getting.

Then, *thirdly*, marriage means *physical union*: 'they will become one flesh'. This certainly includes sexual intercourse, but it involves far more than that. It means that husband and wife will share their whole experience of life, including their pains and disappointments, as well as their joys and pleasures.

Marriage, then, rates very highly in Christian teaching. But the Bible never hints that being single means getting second best. Jesus taught that remaining unmarried is just as much God's gift as being married (see *Matthew* 19:11–12). And Paul echoes that in a very powerful defence of the single life in 1 *Corinthians* 7 (see especially verse 7).

Today, the media try to persuade us that we will only find

complete happiness when we enjoy a physical, sexual relationship. To find out what love is all about, we have to make love first. The Christian gospel labels that kind of propaganda as heresy. Jesus himself did not marry. He never had sexual intercourse. At the end of his life, he was even deserted by his friends. But he (so Christians believe) was the most complete human being who has ever lived. And he knew more about the meaning of love than anyone else ever will.

## Questions for discussion

1. Are Christian principles on sexual behaviour outdated?
2. Is our approach to sex too casual?
3. What has the institution of marriage got to offer modern people? Will it become even less important in the future?

# 6. Divorce

As we saw in the last chapter, the Bible's word for a man and woman 'being united' in marriage really means 'stick'. In this chapter we go on to consider what happens when a marriage becomes 'unstuck'.

No-one wants this to happen. Most would agree that in the best of all possible worlds divorce would not exist. Separation is always painful, even when it relieves the greater pain of a marriage that is already broken. Just as you cannot separate two pieces of paper that have been stuck together, without tearing both of them, so you cannot end a marriage without injuring all those involved — husband, wife, and children too, if there are any.

Divorce statistics are frightening. A recent report by the Study Commission on the Family revealed that one marriage in four now ends in divorce. More than 150 000 children are involved each year, most of them between the ages of five and ten. If you belong to a one-parent family, you are in good company — there are a million of such families in Britain today.

With a failure rate as high as that, you would think that marriage must be a dying institution. Curiously, that does not seem to be the case at all. Even those whose first marriages have failed seem to want to try again. Eight out of ten of those who divorce before the age of 30 remarry within five years. Not all of them get it right the second time, either. The proportion of divorces involving *re*-divorce for one or both partners is rising sharply.

It seems, then, that the comedian was right when he said, 'Marriage is like a besieged city. All those outside want to get in; and all those inside want to get out.'

Why do marriages fail? There are many reasons, but the most powerful one is the growing independence of the individual. This is especially so in the case of women. In Bible times a divorced woman found it difficult to live, unless she remarried.

Today, even with the high unemployment rate, a wife who decides to leave her husband need not fear starvation. If she cannot get a job, there is always social security.

Men, too, are not so helpless without their wives as used to be the case. A divorced man can get his washing done at the launderette, while he slips into the pub for a pint or buys his pre-cooked evening meal at the local supermarket. In other words, the pressures on married people to stick together 'for better, for worse' are far less today than ever before.

## Divorce law

Changes in the law have also eased pressures by making it simpler to get a divorce if you want one. Before the middle of the last century, a man who wanted to end his marriage had to get a special Act of Parliament passed in his favour. There was no other way! In 1857 the Matrimonial Causes Act allowed divorce in cases of adultery, but it was not until 1937 that other grounds were added (including cruelty, desertion and incurable insanity).

The Divorce Reform Act, the law which applies today, came into operation in 1971. It marked a big change in the law's approach to broken marriages. In the past, either husband or wife had to prove that they were the victim of a 'matrimonial offence' (such as adultery, cruelty or desertion). That is not the case any longer. The only ground for divorce in Britain today is 'irretrievable breakdown'. People still say sometimes, 'She got a divorce for adultery', but that is not really so. The court may have accepted her husband's adultery as *evidence* that their marriage was beyond repair, but the only question it is allowed to ask is, 'Has this marriage broken down irretrievably?'

Perhaps the biggest change of all concerns separation. If both husband and wife want a divorce, the court is allowed to accept two years' separation as evidence that their marriage has died. Even if only one partner wants the marriage to end, five years separation is considered evidence enough to overrule the other partner's wishes, and allow the divorce to go through.

## The churches' attitude

The Christian churches are united in their view that marriage should be life-long. They therefore tend to resist all attempts to make divorce easier. When the Divorce Reform Act was passed, the Archbishops of Canterbury and York protested that two years' separation was no proof at all that a marriage relationship had died. The offer of a divorce after so short a time, they said, simply put temptation in the way of couples who would rather take the easy way out than fight through their problems.

Faced with the fact that marriages do break down, however, the churches are divided in their attitudes to divorce and remarriage. Some make allowances for a second start. The Eastern Orthodox Church, for example, is prepared to remarry divorcees. So, too, are most Protestant Free Churches. The local minister is usually given full discretion to take or refuse to take a marriage service if a divorcee is involved, depending on his knowledge of the couple concerned.

The Roman Catholic Church and the Church of England take a stricter view. Neither will permit divorcees to get married in church.

The Roman Catholics do, however, have their own way of allowing some church remarriages to take place. If a divorcee's first marriage is declared null and void, it can, in the church's eyes, simply be ignored. The law of the land also makes provision for nullity, but the church's grounds are far wider than the state's. If, for example, either husband or wife insists on using a contraceptive every time sexual intercourse takes place, the couple have never been properly married, according to the Roman Catholic Church. In the same way, the church authorities may give a couple a decree of nullity if they are satisfied that one or other of them did not understand the implications of marriage on their wedding day.

Roman Catholics recognize several other grounds for nullity, too. So while it is never easy for a Catholic divorcee to 'remarry' in church, he or she can do so if the church authorities can be persuaded that his or her first marriage never really happened.

The Church of England has no such chinks in its armour. A local vicar is legally entitled to marry a divorcee in church, but he is likely to be in trouble with his bishop if he does so. The official Anglican position is that marriage 'involves a moral and spiritual bond which cannot be finally terminated save by death'.

## The nature of marriage

These differences do not just reflect divided church traditions. They arise from contrasting ideas about what marriage is.

Some Christians would say marriage is a *sacrament*. They would claim that every marriage bond is tied by God. No human judge or magistrate has the power to undo it. A divorce decree is therefore as meaningless as a declaration from the Prime Minister that the moon is made of green cheese. Nothing but death can end a marriage. As one Anglican writer has put it, 'A child may be separated from the parent; but the relationship still exists. A husband may be separated from his wife; but only death can dissolve the relationship.'

Seen from this angle, divorce is not just wrong. It is impossible. If a husband divorces and 'remarries', he is committing adultery whenever he goes to bed with his second 'wife'. They are living in sin, because in God's eyes the man will remain married to his former partner until the day she dies.

Others see marriage as a *contract* or a *covenant*. It ought not to be broken, but it can be. The important thing, they tell us, is the couple's relationship. If a married couple grow so far apart that they no longer speak to one another, their relationship is dead. Relationships can wither and die, just like people.

Viewed this way, divorce is like a death certificate. If a marriage is dead, the only thing to do is to give it a proper burial, so a new start can be made. It is a waste of time, as well as living a lie, to pretend that the relationship is alive just because a marriage certificate is tucked away in someone's drawer. And the church's duty is to support the divorcee. If he or she finds another partner, the church can remarry him or her with a clear conscience — or at least provide a service of blessing after a ceremony in the register office.

## The Bible and divorce

The Bible's dislike of divorce is very plain in both the Old Testament and the New. God's ideal for marriage is that it should last for life. No one put it more clearly than the prophet Malachi: ' "I hate divorce", says the Lord God of Israel.' (*Malachi* 2:16)

The apostle Paul, too, was firmly of the view that a married couple belong together 'till death us do part'. 'A married woman', he wrote to the Christians at Rome, 'is bound to her husband as long as he is alive, but if her husband dies, she is released from the law of marriage. So then, if she marries another man while her husband is still alive, she is called an adulteress.' (*Romans* 7:2–3) In putting it so bluntly, Paul was only echoing Jesus' words: 'Anyone who divorces his wife and marries another woman commits adultery against her. And if she divorces her husband and marries another man, she commits adultery.' (*Mark* 10:11–12).

Jesus, however, did not go so far as to ban divorce altogether. On at least two occasions he made an exception in the case of sexual unfaithfulness. 'I tell you', he said, 'that anyone who divorces his wife, *except for marital unfaithfulness*, and marries another woman commits adultery' (*Matthew* 19:9; see also *Matthew* 5:32). He was replying to a question from some Pharisees, who were quizzing him about the Old Testament's allowance for divorce and remarriage (see, for example, *Deuteronomy* 24:1–4). Jesus' answer was, 'Moses permitted you to divorce your wives because your hearts were hard. But it was not this way from the beginning.' (*Matthew* 19:8). In other words, God's creation ideal left no room for divorce at all, but sin's arrival in the world led to breakdown in marriage, and made divorce laws necessary.

Echoing Jesus once again, Paul made a further allowance. He faced a situation in Corinth which Jesus had never faced in Jerusalem. Some marriages were breaking apart because either husbands or wives had become Christians while their partners had not. What should a Christian do in such circumstances? Paul's mind was clear. The Christian must never start divorce proceedings, but 'if the unbeliever leaves, let him do so. A believing man or woman is not bound in such circumstances' (*1 Corinthians* 7:12, 13, 15).

The Bible, then, sets out God's *concession* alongside God's *ideal*. The ideal is high — so high that the disciples once gasped, 'If this is the situation between a husband and wife, it is better not to marry!' (*Matthew* 19:10). But the concession is genuine. In some circumstances (the New Testament mentions sexual unfaithfulness and desertion), married life becomes so bad that divorce is the best of all the bad alternatives. So a policy of easy divorce is wrong, from a biblical point of view, but those who say 'divorce is impossible' run the risk of laying down stricter standards than Christ.

## Questions for discussion

1. Why do you think the divorce rate has risen so dramatically?
2. Are the church's views about divorce too rigid? Should divorcees be allowed to remarry in church if they want to?
3. What extra help and advice should be given:
    (a) to couples who want to get married?
    (b) to married couples who feel their marriages have broken down?

# Work and leisure

## 7. Finding a job

Every school-leaver knows how important it is to find the right
job. Today, most schools offer their senior pupils a great deal of
help in making this vital choice. Careers lessons and work experience schemes are only two of the ways in which bridges are
built between school and the outside world.

It has not always been like that. In the past, many children
drifted into their first jobs with very little thought at all. It was
assumed, very often, that the son would simply follow his father
in the trade or profession that he had inherited from *his* father.
Some small towns were one-industry affairs, and there was very
little else to do if you did not join the pay-roll of the factory, mill
or mine on which the life of the community depended. If you
happened to be a girl, your choices were more limited still.

Even in days of unemployment and restricted job opportunities, the range of careers open to school-leavers is greater today
than ever before. How do you decide which openings to explore?
When all is said and done, there are just three judgements to
make. First, you have to weigh up your own *talents*. What do
you do best? Second, you must make a *choice* of a career which
suits you and matches your abilities. And third, you need to *list*
the relevant job opportunities in your own order of priority.
Which application form will you fill in first?

Christian teaching makes its own distinctive contribution to
all three aspects of job-hunting.

### 1. Talents and gifts

According to the Bible all *my* talents are *God's* gifts. Take, for
example, the direct way the Old Testament describes the crafts-

man's skills as God-given: 'The Lord said . . . "I have chosen Bezalel and I have filled him with my power. I have given him understanding, skill and ability." ' (*Exodus* 31:2–3). The same passage goes on to say that God has also given this man and his colleague 'the ability to teach their crafts to others' (*Exodus* 35:34). And, later on, the prophet Isaiah strikes exactly the same note in tracing the farmer's professional knowledge to God's initiative: 'He knows how to do his work, because God has taught him. All this wisdom comes from the Lord Almighty' (*Isaiah* 28:26, 29).

This is more than an old-fashioned way of saying, 'Some people are naturally good at some things, and some are better at others.' The belief that God is responsible for your natural abilities adds a completely new dimension to job-hunting.

For one thing, it sharpens *ambition*. Turning your back on your talents (or pretending you haven't got any) becomes a much more serious matter if you recognize them as God's gifts. Jesus told his famous parable of the talents to make exactly this point (*Matthew* 25:14–30). The man in the story who hid his gift instead of using it was criticized, not praised. Today, as we know, some people are prevented from using their gifts by lack of suitable job-opportunities. That is a frustrating experience, and not at all the same thing as a lack of ambition.

As the passage quoted above suggests, recognizing your talents as God-given also adds a sense of *service*. If you look on your abilities as a combination of lucky chance, good training and your own hard work, the main question in your mind as you start a career will probably be, 'How can I get to the top fastest?' But your attitude will be rather different if you see your natural abilities as gifts with a purpose. The question at the top of your mind then will be, 'How can I put what I have been given to the best possible use?'

Some careers emphasize the aspect of service more strongly than others. We speak, for example, of 'service industries'. Even the titles of some jobs remind those who do them that their main aim should be to serve others — such as civil *servants*, public *service* employees, and even cabinet *ministers*. Christian teaching lays heavy emphasis on service too. St Paul's job, tent-making, could not really be called a caring occupation, but it was obvious where his priorities lay. As he told other Christian working people at Ephesus, 'I have shown you that by working hard we must help the weak, remembering the words that the Lord Jesus

himself said, "there is more happiness in giving than in receiving".' (*Acts* 20:35)

In Christian terms, *all* jobs are service industries. God is the
giver of all skills and talents. And his purpose in giving them is
to equip ordinary people to serve him through serving one
another.

## 2. Choice and vocation

Most people have the instinctive feeling that somewhere in the
world there is a special small corner with their name on it. Choosing your career means finding a job which is just 'you'.

Christian teaching adds flesh and bones to this instinct. God
does not only love and care for people in a general way, according
to the New Testament. He also has a detailed life-plan for every
individual, which includes career prospects along with everything else. As Paul puts it, 'God has made us what we are, and
in our union with Christ Jesus he has created us for a life of good
deeds, which he has already prepared for us to do.' (*Ephesians*
2:10). Paul's words for 'deeds' there is the usual Bible word for
'work'. Life is like a jigsaw, and work is one piece in it. Finding
the right work is, in Christian terms, finding the piece that exactly
fits — the piece that God the Designer has already prepared.
This does mean, however, that we must broaden our vision of
work itself, especially in days of high unemployment. 'Having
work' is not quite the same thing as 'having a paid job'. See
Chapter 8 for further ideas about that.

A word often used in this connection is *vocation*. It simply
means 'calling', and reflects the belief that God 'calls' individual
people to particular occupations. Sometimes God's call results in
dramatic changes. Amos, for example, was out fruit-picking
when God called him to move north and become a prophet (*Amos*
7:14–15). Simon and Andrew were fishing when Jesus called out
from the shore, 'Come with me, and I will teach you to catch
men.' According to Matthew, 'at once they left their nets and
went with him' (*Matthew* 4:18–20) — which must have been quite
a shock to the others in the family business.

Such sudden and dramatic events were as rare in Bible times,
however, as they are today. Most of the work in the Roman
world of New Testament days was done by slaves. Though some
of their jobs were more interesting than we might imagine (your
doctor, in those times, would probably have been a slave, as

would your private secretary and the stage star you went to watch on a Saturday evening for your entertainment), they had no freedom to choose their careers. Yet the New Testament has no hesitation in encouraging them to look upon their work as God's calling (see *1 Corinthians* 7:20–24). Even a slave's forced labour was a vocation.

It is, in fact, a basic Christian belief that every person has a vocation, in the sense that there is something specific that God wants him or her to do in life. In Christian terms, therefore, choosing your career means discovering what God is calling you to do. The average person will not see letters of gold on the bedroom wall saying 'chartered accountant' or 'typist'. Guidance usually comes in far more ordinary ways — especially through getting careers advice and recognizing the talents which (as we have seen) are really God's gifts.

### 3. Choosing the best

The logical conclusion of the last section is that God's calling — whatever it is — will always be the best choice. If you are convinced that becoming a computer programmer is your own proper vocation, then that is the best possible choice of career *for you.*

It would be quite wrong, of course, to go on to say that computer programming should be *everyone's* first choice, or to draw up a 'Best Jobs' league table with computer programming at the top and everything else underneath it.

However stupid that may sound, it has long been common practice to value some jobs above others. In the Middle Ages, the church even did it with the idea of vocation itself. If you became a monk or a nun, said church leaders, you had a 'vocation', but if you opted for any other career you ended up with just an 'ordinary job'. Seeing how this contradicted the teaching of the New Testament, the sixteenth-century Reformers spoke out strongly against it. But they did so at the risk of their lives. One of them, the Englishman William Tyndale, was actually executed for heresy partly because he taught that 'there is no work better than another to please God; to pour water, to wash dishes, to be a cobbler or an apostle is one; to wash dishes and to preach is all one, to please God.'

Old ideas die hard, and even today it would be unusual to hear a road sweeper or an office cleaner describe their jobs as vocations. Most of us, in fact, have our own private league tables of jobs. We may look down on unskilled labour as beneath us, or we may despise pen-pushers in offices as people who do not know what real work is because they never get their hands dirty. Either way, this kind of discrimination is something totally alien to Christian teaching.

In biblical times, manual work was generally considered to be at the very bottom of the jobs list. It is all the more remarkable, therefore, to find the Old Testament describing God as a manual worker. The universe is 'the work of his fingers', sings the Psalmist (*Psalms* 8:3). The Creator works elbow-deep in his raw material like a potter with his clay (*Isaiah* 45:9). According to the creation story, God even had his rest day and enjoyed job satisfaction when he looked back on what he had done at the end of his working week (*Genesis* 1:31, 2:2–3).

Jesus, too, was a manual worker. His friends knew him as 'just a carpenter' (*Mark* 6:3), and in those days — before the invention of power tools — carpentry was a muscle-building trade. So hard, physical labour was not beneath the dignity of the Son of God, however much it was despised by the average Greek or Roman of his time.

The New Testament as well as the Old, therefore, discourages us strongly from cataloguing jobs in some order of value. It is an important part of Christian teaching that all work has the same status. St Paul uses the human body to drive this point home. It is the parts of our bodies that we despise and reject most, he points out, that really perform the most vital functions. One cannot say to another, 'I'm not needed', or — worse still — 'You're not wanted' (see *1 Corinthians* 12:14–26).

To sum up, then, the Christian approach to job-hunting is distinctive in three ways. It encourages us to think of our talents and abilities as God's gifts. It invites us to interpret our choice of career as God's call to us. And it underlines the value of what we are called to do, by insisting that all jobs are equally worthwhile.

## Questions for discussion

1. Is enough being done to bridge the gap between school and the outside world?

*Time on your hands. Being out of work and bored is a soul-destroying way of life. Can you say exactly why, and imagine what the effects might be?*

2. How important is it to find the right job?
3. What would attract you to a job? How far would you be
   influenced by Christian principles in deciding what to do?

# 8. Attitudes to work

What is your attitude to work? Your feelings are probably mixed.
Ask a typical group of working people what they think about
their jobs, and the replies will probably vary from 'we hate it' to
'we love it'.

The most popular answer might be 'we don't like it, but we
put up with it'. Work, as many people see it, is a necessary evil.
It is the only way there is for most of us to earn the money we
need to do the things we really want to do. So a 'good' job is one
that provides as much pay as possible for as little work as
possible.

Seen in this light, unemployment can look quite attractive
— if, of course, the size of our social security benefits allows us
to enjoy our leisure time. Curiously, though, those who cannot
find jobs feel they are losing more than fat wage-packets. The
magazine *New Society* recently carried out a survey among the
unemployed, and only a very few of them complained about lack
of money. Most of them put things such as boredom, aimlessness
and a sense of rejection at the top of their complaints list.

One teenager who was interviewed said, 'I just stay at home,
which is so boring and depressing because all I want to do is to
go to work.' Another, when he was asked what he did with his
time, replied that spare time was different now he was off work.
When he was working he came home in the evenings, had a
meal and sat down and watched television, because he was tired.
But since he was not working, he said, 'You find yourself getting
up later and later. Now I have trouble in getting out of my bed
before 10 o'clock in the morning. It comes on after a while — you
know there's nothing to do, so you stay in bed most of the time.'

Strangely enough, comments like those from the jobless come
much closer to a Christian approach to work than the attitude of
the employed person who sees his or her job as a bore and a
nuisance. Christian teaching does, in fact, have a very positive
outlook on work. To find out more about it, we need to ask two

basic questions. First, *What is work?*; and second, *What is work for?*

## What is work?

According to the first book of the Bible, work is *management of the created world*. When God made man and woman, he said to them 'Have many children, so that your descendants will live all over the earth and bring it under control.' (*Genesis* 1:28). The story of creation does not describe Paradise as a holiday camp or a rest centre! Adam was given a most demanding job to do — in modern terms, a combination of estate management and agricultural labour. (*Genesis* 2:15)

It may seem strange to go back to the book of Genesis in order to find light on the twentieth century's problems, but this is where a Christian approach to work begins. Man's commission to bring the world's resources under control covers everything we label as 'work' today, all the way from scientific research and technological development to housekeeping and social welfare. And that simple instruction from God the Creator gives modern people two vital guidelines in discovering the place work should have in their lives.

(i) *Work is part of being human.*   The fact that God made man and woman as workers tells us that this is the way people are meant to be. Take away from any person the chance to work, and you have made him or her just a little sub-human. As a professor of theology once put it, 'To be denied the opportunity of work is to be treated as something less than a human being.'

The unemployed reflect this aspect of Christian teaching when they complain of boredom and apathy. People were never meant to live through long, boring days filled with nothing. In the words of one Christian sociologist, 'to become unemployed can be a great blow to a man: it is not just the loss of earning power, but also the concept of being a man that is attacked.'

This goes a long way towards explaining why there are twice as many attempted suicides among the unemployed as there are among people with jobs. The plasterer who complained that being made redundant was 'like somebody cutting your throat' was echoing the very high value Christianity puts on work. Being deprived of it is, in the Bible's view, very similar to experiencing an attack on your life.

This explains, too, why the Bible condemns laziness so strongly. 'How long is the lazy man going to lie in bed?', asks the Old Testament angrily. 'When is he ever going to get up?' (*Proverbs* 6:9). St Paul had a simple answer: 'He who does not work shall not eat' (2 *Thessalonians* 3:10). Those who depend on others, instead of working to support themselves, need to be taught a sharp lesson — for their own good, as well as for everyone else's.

Some people conclude from this that the Bible is against paying social security benefits to the unemployed. But that is a false conclusion. Paul's blunt words were aimed at people who could get work but preferred to avoid it. Despite the suggestions that are sometimes made, very few unemployed people are work-shy. Most would gladly give up their place in the dole queue for a job that would make them financially independent.

(ii) *Work is not the same as employment.* This is the second guideline the Bible's creation teaching offers us. Management of the created world adds up to far more than a list of paid jobs.

Here, perhaps, is the biggest contribution a Christian view of work can make to the modern unemployment debate. Whatever the politicians say, the rate of unemployment is likely to rise, as new technology makes more and more people redundant. Computers and other electronic gadgets will do more efficiently and far more quickly the jobs that men and women are being paid to do now. Some experts predict that the average person in the twenty-first century will only be able to expect a three-day working week for an eight-year working life. What will that do to our outlook on work and leisure?

If we think 'work' means 'a paid job', the outlook is bad. Society will be saying to more and more people, 'We have no jobs for you. You are therefore useless. We will pay you something, but you are worth nothing.'

If, however, we think of our work as something far bigger than a job for which we get paid, the picture changes dramatically. Already a great deal of valuable work is being done by people who earn no wages for doing it. Millions of women have full-time unpaid 'jobs' in the home. Other people do some kind of voluntary work, such as leading youth clubs, with nothing more than their expenses in return for their effort. Even the retired have an important, though less obvious, contribution to make, by sharing their wisdom and experience.

All these things come under the heading of 'work', as the Bible defines it. All contribute in a useful way to the management of creation's resources. Whether or not they attract a wage does not really matter, as far as their value is concerned. There may well be far fewer wage-earning jobs in the future than there have been in the past. Far more people than ever before may be receiving some kind of social benefit. But, in Christian terms, that will simply release them for more creative occupations which are just as much 'work' as jobs of the more traditional kind.

**What is work for?**

Assuming you have work to do, the next important question to ask is, 'Why do you do it?'

Different people would give different answers. 'Money' is the most obvious one, but there are others too. Some work hard to get the extra power and influence that promotion brings. Others look for security. And there are those who go on searching until they find a job that will give them personal satisfaction — even if the wages are low and the prospects uncertain.

There is a big difference between working for some*thing* (such as money, power or security) and working for some*one*. Apart from wives and mothers, who work at home out of love for their husbands and children, there are not many jobs where the focus is on pleasing people. Modern working conditions certainly contribute to this. Employees are often treated as tools, and they react accordingly. If you work on a production line or in a typing pool, it is hard to think of yourself as working for a *person*. If the firm is a multi-national, you will probably never even know who your real boss is.

From a Christian point of view, this 'depersonalizing' of work is wrong. 'To mistreat the workman as "a piece of machinery" is a violation of his human dignity', wrote Abraham Kuyper, the famous Dutch political commentator. 'Even worse, it is a sin going squarely against the sixth commandment, thou shalt not kill.'

The New Testament certainly strikes a very personal note when it answers the question, 'What is work for?' Paul wrote like this to Christian workers in the town of Colossae: 'Whatever you do, work at it with all your heart, as though you were working for the Lord and not for men.' (*Colossians* 3:23) Given that insight of faith, there will be no problems over quality control. Every piece of work will be done well if it is done for Christ, and not just to pass the supervisor's scrutiny. In another of his letters, Paul puts it even more strongly: 'Don't work hard only when your master is watching and then shirk when he isn't looking; work hard and with gladness all the time, as though working for Christ.' (*Ephesians* 6:6–7)

This, of course, is a distinctively Christian incentive. You need eyes of faith to see beyond the boss to Jesus Christ! Nevertheless, it does not take faith to see that work done for someone you know and admire will be done that much better. Some time ago a London paper carried a photograph of a boy cleaning a pair of boots. He was obviously doing the job with enormous enthusiasm and care. The caption underneath explained why. The boots belonged to the goalkeeper of the boy's favourite football team. He was doing a rotten job for no money at all because of the person who had asked him to do it.

The conditions of working life have, of course, changed greatly from biblical times to our own day. Paul was not writing to trade union members but to slaves, who did most of the work in the ancient Roman world. Even Jesus' picture of the good shepherd and his flock does not really fit the job description of a modern Australian sheep-farmer rearing and marketing his thousands of animals. We have, therefore, to be very cautious in applying biblical teaching to modern working problems.

Nevertheless, Sir Fred Catherwood was reflecting the views of many industrialists when, as chairman of the National Economic Development Council, he appealed for a return to the New Testament's stress on the importance of personal relationships at work. 'The problems of this age are not technical', he wrote. 'If you look at the economy of any country and you begin to probe the reasons for slow progress, you very quickly discover that the reasons are not technical but human.'

## Questions for discussion

1. How important an aspect of life is a paid job?
2. What do you hope to gain from your work?
3. How far is unemployment to blame for the increasing violence in society? What more can be done to help the unemployed?

# 9. Attitudes to money

Most people spend a great deal of time thinking about money. When they are not dreaming up new ways to get rich, they are working out better ways of using the little they have. Unless we are already either millionaires or nuns, money probably comes very high on our list of priorities.

**Better off without it?**

The New Testament's teaching on money is revolutionary. Sometimes Jesus even seems to be saying that people are better off without it. 'It is much harder for a rich person to enter the Kingdom of God', he once said, 'than for a camel to go through the eye of a needle' (*Mark* 10:25). Mark reports that the disciples were 'shocked at these words' and 'amazed'. No wonder! They had assumed, as many people do today, that being rich is an important part of being successful.

Again and again in the Gospels we find Jesus hitting the same note. He told one well-off young man, 'Go and sell all you have and give the money to the poor' (*Mark* 10:21). When he sent his disciples out to spread his message, he ordered them to travel light, with no money in their pockets (*Mark* 6:8). And the first Christians clearly took him at his word. They had a casual attitude to the things they owned. 'No-one said that any of his belongings was his own', comments Luke, 'but they all shared with one another everything they had. There was no-one in the group who was in need. Those who owned fields or houses would sell them, bring the money received from the sale, and hand it over to the apostles, and the money was distributed to each one according to his need'. (*Acts* 4:32, 34–35).

It would be quite wrong to conclude, however, that all Christians who take Jesus at his word today should be penniless. He never taught that himself. Nor does the rest of the Bible. The Ten Commandments' ban on stealing, for example, makes no sense at all if God's people are not meant to own anything. The point Jesus made had nothing to do with *amounts* of money. He was far more concerned with people's *attitudes* to what they have.

## The wrong attitude

In particular, he exposed the root of all wrong attitudes, as he saw it. Make money into your god, he taught, and you cannot possibly live as a Christian. 'No-one can be a slave of two masters; he will hate one and love the other; he will be loyal to one and despise the other. You cannot serve both God and Money.' (*Matthew* 6:24). It is in this light that we are meant to understand his instruction to the rich young man to sell everything. Here was a wealthy person who had surrendered his life to his money. He had allowed his possessions to possess him. The moment of truth came when he turned away sadly from Jesus' challenge.

Paul captured Jesus' meaning exactly when he wrote, 'the love of money' (notice, not money itself) 'is a source of all kinds of evil' (*1 Timothy* 6:10). 'Those who are rich', he went on, should worship not their wealth but their God 'who richly gives us everything for our enjoyment' (verse 17). In other words, money makes a good servant, but a bad master. That conviction lies right at the heart of the Christian approach to wealth and possessions.

Jesus obviously thought this was a vital part of his teaching, because he often stopped to demonstrate the dangers of a money-centred lifestyle. In his parables, especially, he spelled out the many different ways money can poison life.

(a) *At the personal level*, he taught, putting money first can harm people in two opposite ways. They may never have enough to buy what they want, in which case they 'start worrying: "Where will my food come from? Or my drink? Or my clothes?" '. Nine times out of ten that kind of worry means they are attaching too much importance to the things money can buy. 'After all', (Jesus went on) 'Isn't life worth more than food? And isn't the body worth more than clothes? Can any of you live a bit longer by worrying about it?' (*Matthew* 6:25, 27, 31).

On the other hand, there are those like the farmer in Jesus' parable who did so well that he decided on an early retirement. In his case, having more than enough of the things money could buy lulled him into a false sense of security. No sooner had he said to himself, 'Lucky man! You have all the good things you need for many years. Take life easy, eat, drink and enjoy yourself!', than God intervened: 'You fool! This very night you will have to give up your life; then who will get all those things you have kept for yourself?' If death is the end, the rich man can rest content with the prospect of an elaborate funeral. But if there is an after-life, as Jesus claimed, selfish hoarding begins to look very stupid indeed (*Luke* 12:16–21).

(b) *At the social level*, Jesus taught that putting money first can blind people to the needs of others. In today's language, how can a man contribute generously to famine relief if his mind is set on paying for an extension to his garage so he can get a bigger car?

This theme comes across most vividly in the story of the rich man and the beggar. Basking in his luxury, the rich man ignores the sore-covered beggar on his doorstep who survives on the leftovers from his banquet. It is his selfishness that seals his fate, not his wealth (*Luke* 16:19–31). And Jesus drove home this point in a terrifying way when he predicted God's final day of judgement. There will be those, he said, whom God will condemn not because they have done anyone any harm, but because they have failed to use their money to help others (*Matthew* 25:41–46).

(c) *At the spiritual level*, Jesus warned his disciples in the strongest terms that making an idol out of money would cut their lines of communication with God. 'The love for riches chokes the message', he explained after telling them the parable of the Sower. Just as weeds throttle the life out of growing corn, so the love of money stunts the spiritual growth of Christian people. God gets crowded out when making and spending money are put first (*Matthew* 13:22).

### The right attitude

These blunt warnings are the most striking feature of Jesus' teaching on money. But there is another side to the picture, too. Alongside his exposure of wrong attitudes, he was careful to sketch in the outline of right ones. As well as laying bare the root of the wrong (making money into an idol), he also highlighted the starting-point for the right.

All right attitudes to money, Jesus taught, spring from the

conviction that every person is just a trustee of what he or she has. God alone is the owner. Even when people earn their money by hard work, the Bible reminds its readers that both their talents and their resources are God-given. The Old Testament is particularly vivid in stressing this fact of life. 'The world and all that is in it belong to the Lord', sang King David (*Psalms* 24:1). 'Everything in heaven and earth is yours, all riches and wealth come from you.' (*1 Chronicles* 29:11–12).

This, too, is the main point Jesus wanted to get across in his story about the investment money (*Matthew* 25:14–30). All three of the servants in that parable were entrusted with different amounts of the master's money. It remained his, but they were held responsible for the way it was used. And it was the trustee who mismanaged his resources, by failing to use them properly, who earned the owner's anger.

Just as the Bible spells out the consequences of idolizing money, it also sets out the value of using it rightly.

(a) *At the personal level*, Christians who see themselves as trustees, not owners, avoid the twin dangers of anxiety and complacency. Instead of having their inward peace ruined by worry about not having enough, they learn to depend on God for everything they need. 'He will provide you with these things', promised Jesus (*Luke* 12:31). And Paul, for one, found immense satisfaction in that promise. 'I know what it is to be in need and what it is to have more than enough', he wrote. 'I have learned this secret, so that anywhere, at any time, I am content whether I am full or hungry, whether I have too much or too little.' (*Philippians* 4:11–12).

It is Paul, too, who signposts the wealthy away from a false sense of security. The rich, he says, are 'not to be proud, but to place their hope, not in such an uncertain thing as riches, but in God.' (*1 Timothy* 6:17). In other words, the more money Christians have, the greater their responsibility to God and the bigger their reasons for remembering that 'they can't take it with them when they go'.

(b) *At the social level*, this 'trustee' attitude to money spells an end to selfishness. Jesus encouraged his disciples to use their resources to meet other people's practical needs, instead of hanging on to what they had in a tight-fisted way and grudging every penny given to persistent charity collectors. The first Christians quickly gained a world-wide reputation for generosity. One Roman Emperor even complained rather peevishly, 'The godless Galileans nourish *our* poor in addition to their own; while ours get no care from us.'

Even Paul was amazed by the happy, open-hearted way the churches he knew parted with their money. Writing about one congregation, he said 'Somehow, in most difficult circumstances, their joy and the fact of being down to their last penny themselves produced a magnificent concern for other people. I can guarantee that they were willing to give to the limit of their means, yes and beyond their means, without the slightest urging from me or anyone else.' (*2 Corinthians* 8:2–3).

Later in the same letter, Paul made it quite clear that he knew the reason for such generosity. 'After all', he wrote, 'God can give you everything you need, so that you may always have sufficient both for yourselves and for giving away to other people. The more you are enriched by God the more scope will there be for generous giving.' (*2 Corinthians* 9:8, 11).

(c) *At the spiritual level*, those who recognize that they are God's trustees (not owners) of all they have find many valuable outlets for their money in his service. Instead of coming between him and them, their possessions become aids to worship — like Mary's expensive perfume and the poor widow's small change (*John* 12:3, *Luke* 21:1–3).

Again it is Paul who puts this into words most clearly: 'your giving does not end in meeting the wants of your fellow-Christians. It also results in an overflowing tide of thanksgiving to God. Moreover, your very giving proves the reality of your faith, and that means that men thank God that you practise the gospel that you profess to believe in, as well as for the actual gifts you make to them and to others.' (*2 Corinthians* 9:12–13).

Unlike many of the subjects we are considering, this is one on which we can simply let the Bible speak for itself. In a nutshell, Christian teaching on money focuses on attitudes, not amounts. A life dominated by money is always wrong (whether the sums involved are big or small). The right attitude, as taught by Jesus, is for a person to accept what he or she has as a trust from God. In practical terms this means depending on him for life's necessities, and looking for his way to spend anything extra — with the needs of those who are worse off especially in mind.

## Questions for discussion

1. To what extent are our attitudes towards money influenced by the outside world (e.g., T.V., films and advertisements)?
2. Does being wealthier automatically mean being happier? Can you think of cases where this is not so?
3. Do you agree with the way Jesus described *right* attitudes to money?

# 10. Attitudes to leisure

If this book had been written 50 years ago, the theme of leisure would never have found a place on the contents page. Nor would it have featured in examination question papers! The fact that it now does both reflects two important changes that have taken place in modern social life. In the first place, working hours have been reduced, so the average person has more leisure time to spend. And secondly, the importance of the part leisure activities play in our lives is being more and more clearly recognized.

The reduction of working hours has been a gradual process. The micro-chip revolution and the threat of increasing unemployment have focused our attention on it sharply in recent years, but it was our great-great-grandfathers who felt the greatest impact of the change. Between 1820 and 1918, the standard working week was reduced by a third — from 72 hours to 48.

Today, we see evidence of the booming leisure industry all around us. Bookmakers, T.V. rental companies and shops selling records, sports equipment and do-it-yourself materials compete for the best sites in our High Streets. Recent British government surveys have revealed that the average family spends more than a quarter of its annual budget on leisure — and that *excludes* money spent on travel. So the question is being asked more and more seriously: if leisure activities have become such a prominent feature of modern life, should we not be giving much more care and attention to the way we spend our leisure time?

The Christian contribution to the debate on leisure begins at the point we left our discussion about work.

## An all-life view

In Chapter 7 we explored the meaning of *vocation*, as the key to understanding the Christian approach to work. We discovered, among other things, that it was wrong to classify our work as either 'a vocation' or 'an ordinary job'. Because 'vocation' means 'calling', and because God calls everyone to do something in life, it is a basic Christian principle that everybody has a vocation, whatever the job he or she does.

Now, as the focus shifts from work to leisure, we have to push back the boundaries of vocation further still. Only very rarely in the Bible do we find God calling men and women to *do* particular jobs. Far more often he calls people to *be* something for him, in the *whole* of their lives. Paul sums it up when he writes to the Christians at Thessalonica, 'We ask our God to make you worthy of the *life* he has called you to live' (2 *Thessalonians* 1:11; compare *Ephesians* 4:1).

In other words, the Bible presents vocation as an all-life affair. It extends to every part of our lives, not just to our jobs. It covers our leisure activities just as much as our work. In Christian terms, teachers do not take a holiday from their vocation on the last day of the school term, any more than typists abandon their vocation for the week-end when they cover their typewriters and lock their offices.

The modern tendency to divide life into compartments labelled 'work' and 'leisure' is not one that we find reflected in Christian teaching. It is, in fact, very hard to make such a hard-and-fast distinction at all, when you come to work it out in practice. If, for example, you regard work as something you get paid for and leisure as everything else, you have trouble in accounting for people such as schoolchildren and housewives. Are studying for exams and making beds really leisure activities? Similar problems arise if you label work as exertion and leisure as relaxation. What about the supermarket cashier who sits pressing buttons from Monday to Friday and trains for marathons at week-ends?

One practical result of seeing life as all of a piece is that our approach to leisure (whatever it is!) becomes positive and constructive. If my leisure-time is part of my total vocation, it will take on the qualities of purpose and direction. Instead of drifting through 'spare time' aimlessly, I will plan it in the conviction that my whole life (of which leisure is an important part) is on the move to a positive goal. And that is a powerful antidote to boredom.

At this point Christian teaching differs quite sharply from the usual approach to leisure-time today. One dictionary, for example, defines leisure as 'freedom from occupation or business; time free from employment'. The Christian view is more positive than that. It thinks in terms of being freed *for* certain purposes, rather than being freed *from* particular chores.

**Major and minor**

If we ask what distinctions the Bible makes in the use of time, we arrive very quickly at the *sabbath principle*. That is spelled out in the fourth of the Ten Commandments: 'Observe the Sabbath and keep it holy. You have six days in which to do your work, but the seventh day is a day of rest dedicated to me. On that day no-one is to work.' (*Exodus* 20:8–10).

We tend to link the idea of sabbath with the Christian Sunday and to equate its observance with church-going. That, however, limits the meaning of the word far too narrowly. 'Sabbath' simply means 'stopping', and 'keeping it holy' means 'making it special'. In the Bible, when God declared something holy, he took it out of ordinary circulation. So the sabbath day was primarily a special day when a man or woman's usual activity was temporarily suspended.

The way in which the sabbath principle is worked out in the rest of the Bible shows that the vital keynote is *change*. 'Work' stood for a person's usual occupation (whether or not he or she was paid for it). The sabbath law, therefore, demanded that at regular intervals everyone should have a change from what they usually did. Out in the desert, the Israelites were told to stay in their tents on the sabbath day, because that was the only major change they could make in their way of life at the time (*Exodus* 16:29). In more settled circumstances, the regulations became more specific: the farmer must stop his ploughing, the housewife must take a break from her housework and the travelling sales-man must put his samples down (*Exodus* 34:21, 35:3; *Jeremiah* 17:27).

The applications varied, but the principle remained the same. The 'major' element in every person's life (normally, though not always, his or her job) must be balanced by a 'minor' element, when he or she deliberately did something else.

The exact proportion of major to minor becomes less import-ant as we move from the Old Testament to the New. Paul, for example, criticized Christians who insisted on observing the six-to-one ratio of the Old Testament law too slavishly (see *Co-lossians* 2:16). But the need for a regular change is still stressed. Even Jesus, who made religious leaders furious by the way he sat loosely to the details of their sabbath rules and regulations, saw to it that his disciples had breaks from their work (see, for example, *Mark* 6:31).

The Bible, then, has a very high view of leisure. Unfortunately, the Christian Church has not always matched it. The Puritans, especially, tended to frown on all leisure activities as sheer idleness. 'If vain recreation, dressings, feastings, idle talk, unprofitable company or sleep be any of them temptations to rob you of any of your time', warned Richard Baxter, 'accordingly heighten your watchfulness.' Baxter and his fellow-Puritans were right in stressing the value of work, but in doing so they undermined the value of leisure. The sabbath principle of the Bible rules out all 'workaholic' attitudes which destroy the balance between the major and the minor elements of life.

For this reason Christians are understandably cautious in supporting the repeal of the old British 'Sunday laws'. Many of these regulations are now out-dated, but their purpose was a good one — to stop anyone from having to work a seven-day week. As these regulations fall into disuse, or get by-passed, some working people become particularly vulnerable.

Many professional cricketers, for example, find themselves without a day off during the season, now that the John Player League has taken over their Sundays. When Sunday play in the English Football League was first suggested, some players and officials protested for similar reasons, and not only on their own behalf. As a general manager of one First Division club put it, 'We do not think it is fair to upset a rest day for so many people. Why should police and transport workers be called on for extra work? They should be allowed to relax on Sundays.' That expressed the Bible's sabbath principle very well, even though the manager was quick to add, 'Our decision has nothing to do with religion.'

**Purposes**

If, then, opportunities for change are so important, and if leisure is part of God's calling, how can people structure their leisure time in the best positive way? The Bible has two guidelines to offer.

(i) *Service*: One of the purposes behind the Old Testament's sabbath day laws was that a person's rest period should benefit others (see, for example, *Deuteronomy* 5:14). By Jesus' time this humanitarian aim had sunk without trace in the sea of rules about prohibited sabbath activities. Jesus deliberately set out to resurrect it, especially by healing the sick on the sabbath. Once he called a man with a paralysed hand to the front of the synagogue congregation. 'What does our Law allow us to do on the Sabbath?', he asked. 'To help or to harm? To save a man's life or to destroy it?' When he got no answer, Mark tells us that he 'was angry as he looked round on them, but at the same time he felt sorry for them, because they were so stubborn and wrong'. (*Mark* 3:1–5).

For Jesus, then, a day of rest was a particularly appropriate time for serving others. In today's language, leisure time offers opportunities for welfare service which Christians will be eager to seize. The details, of course, will vary from person to person and from place to place, but the principle means that a Christian's approach to leisure will, above everything else, be unselfish. Following through Jesus' teaching, Paul tells the Corinthians that the first question to be asked about any activity is not, 'Where's the harm in it?' but 'How will it help?'. 'No one should be looking to his own interests', he concludes, 'but to the interests of others.' (*1 Corinthians* 10:23–24).

(ii) *Wholeness*: Jesus promised his disciples, 'I have come in order that you might have life — life in all its fulness.' (*John* 10:10). And he demonstrated what he meant by 'fulness' in the way he dealt with other people. The four Gospel-writers tell us how he healed sick bodies, brought peace and sanity to tortured minds, and met spiritual needs. So the 'full' life that Jesus promised was a life touched in every part (body, mind and soul) by his power.

This concern on Jesus' part that people should live full lives provides a useful pointer for structuring leisure time. The Christian principle which emerges is that our leisure activities should combine with our work to make us 'whole' people. Kenneth Greet, a Methodist writer, spells it out in practical terms like this: 'If our work involves no physical exercise, our leisure should include it. If our work excludes the possibility of developing personal relationships, time for this should be found in leisure. Conversely, if our work is largely spent with people, we should try in part of our leisure to experience being alone. For most people work includes no sense of worship and may lack the

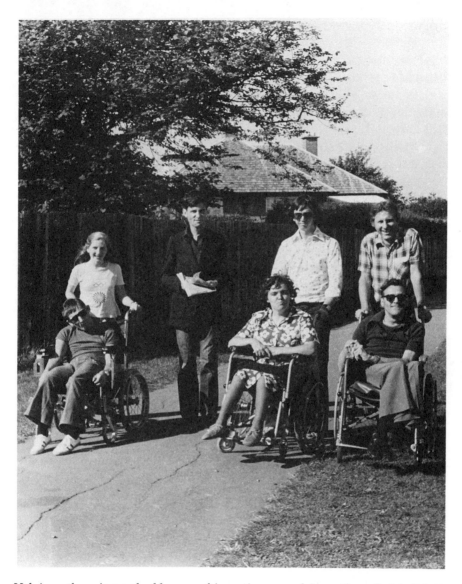

*Helping others is a valuable way of investing some leisure time. But is it just to give yourself a 'good' feeling? What might your motives be? And who benefits most?*

opportunity for service. These things, then, should be part of our leisure.'

That last point — the need to worship — is one that Jesus himself often made. In his view, no one can be properly 'whole' unless he or she worships God. A life full of work and leisure activities is still unbalanced and incomplete, in Christian terms, if it leaves the spiritual dimension empty.

Finally, Jesus showed both in his teaching and by his example that a full life means a life spent enjoying ordinary things. People constantly criticized him for enjoying himself too much, (see, for example, *Luke* 5:33–35). He turned water into wine at a wedding reception (*John* 2:1–11), and was slandered by some as 'a glutton and a heavy drinker' (*Matthew* 11:19). He accepted the kind of invitations that other religious people refused (*Luke* 5:29–30). Even when he was near the time of his death, he told his disciples that the object of his teaching was 'that my joy may be in you and that your joy may be complete.' (*John* 15:11).

A positive approach to leisure time is not the same as an intense approach to life which despises pleasure. The famous evangelist John Wesley once fell into this trap when he founded a school and made one of its rules, 'There will be no games, for he that plays when a boy will play when a man.' Though the New Testament warns its readers against idolizing pleasure (in *1 Corinthians* 6:12, for example) it takes a very positive view of all the enjoyable things which help to make people whole. After all, Paul reminds his young friend Timothy, it is 'God who richly provides us with everything for our enjoyment' (*1 Timothy* 6:17).

## Questions for discussion

1. Do you think the role of leisure will become more important in the future? If so, why?
2. How necessary is it to plan your leisure time, if you are to gain the full benefit from it?
3. Do you agree with the Christian view that your leisure time should be spent doing something to make your life 'whole'?

# *Part D*
# Society's casualties

## 11. Community service

From its earliest days, the Christian church gained a big reputation for social care and welfare. The first Christians spent an enormous amount of time and money looking after society's outcasts, from abandoned children to the unwanted elderly. They visited the sick, helped those in prison, provided hospitality for travellers and found work for the unemployed. 'For those able to work, provide work', Bishop Cyprian commanded his congregation (A.D. 250); 'to those incapable, be charitable'.

Often, help was given at great risk to the donors. Dionysius of Alexandria (A.D. 250) tells how many Christians died after fearlessly caring for the sick, when a plague struck the city. 'Quite the reverse was it with the heathen', he comments, 'who fled from their dearest friends and threw out their sick half-dead.' In Rome, church members went to amazing lengths to help prisoners. Clement, a prominent Christian leader in the city (A.D. 100) tells how 'many have given themselves up to be captives in order to ransom others; many have sold themselves into slavery to feed others.'

The Early Church certainly earned its reputation the hard way. The historian Eusebius (A.D 325) described the impact of Christian welfare during an outbreak of contagious sickness like this: 'Christians showed themselves at that time to all the heathen in the most brilliant light; for the Christians were the only people who, in the midst of so much and so great tribulation, proved by deeds their sympathy and love. Some busied themselves day after day with the care and burial of dead bodies (they were without number, and no one else bothered about them); others gathered together into one place all who were tortured by hunger and supplied them with food. When this became known, people glorified the God of the Christians, and confessed that they alone were the truly pious and God-fearing people, because they gave proof of it by their deeds.'

Even in these early days, however, some Christians opted out of society altogether. One hermit lived all by himself on top of Mount Sinai for 50 years. He refused to see any visitors because, he said, 'the man who is often visited by mortals cannot be visited by angels.' Another, Simeon Stylites (A.D. 420), built himself a pillar and lived on top of it for 36 years to escape human contact (though, to be fair, he did attract great admiration for his sermons, which were delivered from 60 feet above the heads of his audiences!).

This 'world-denying' tradition has persisted in the church, but only as an alternative lifestyle for the few. Throughout its history, the life of the mainstream church has been marked by energetic involvement in the needs of the community. If you dig below the surface of any government-sponsored welfare agency today, you will probably find, at its root, some church-based voluntary service organization. Free schooling, children's and old people's homes, trade associations and hostels for the homeless all began this way.

## Covenant care

The origin of Christian social concern pre-dates the coming of Jesus. His second great commandment ('Love your neighbour as yourself', *Mark* 12:31) was taken straight from the pages of the Old Testament covenant law, and it was the covenant that provided the Jews of Jesus' time with their greatest stimulus to get involved in society's needs.

'Covenant' simply means 'agreement', but in Old Testament times the word conveyed a far richer, warmer meaning than the legal wording of a will or a hire-purchase agreement today. The Old Testament covenant sealed the relationship of love that God had made with his people. And on their side, it demanded obedience to his laws, as a grateful response to his love.

These laws set out Israel's social obligations in great detail. And prominent among them were rules for the care of the community's weakest members. Widows, orphans and immigrants are mentioned particularly frequently (see, for example, *Exodus* 22:21–24). Even the physically disabled get the law's special protection. Shouting insults at the deaf and setting up traps for the blind are not just harmless practical jokes. They anger the God of the covenant, whose love has a special place for the weak (see *Leviticus* 19:14).

God's love very often provides the main incentive for social concern in the Old Testament. 'He makes sure that orphans and widows are treated fairly', the law explains; 'he loves the foreigners who live with our people, and gives them food and clothes. *So then*, show love for those foreigners.' (*Deuteronomy* 10:18–19). 'If you take someone's cloak as a pledge that he will pay you, you must give it back to him before the sun sets, because it is the only covering he has to keep him warm. What else can he sleep in? When he cries out to me for help, I will answer him *because I am merciful.*' (Exodus 22:26–27).

The covenant's bond, then, had a two-way effect. As well as fixing the individual's eyes on God and his laws, it also tied the interests of individuals to one another's needs. One repeated phrase summed up the closeness people felt within the covenant community, and the sense of responsibility they accepted for one another. According to the story of creation in Genesis, when Eve was brought to Adam, he exclaimed 'This is now bone of my bone and flesh of my flesh' (*Genesis* 2:23). A long time later, a man called Abimelech used exactly the same phrase of his extended family (see *Judges* 9:1–2). And later still, the whole nation of Israel described their relationship with David, their political leader, in the same words yet again. 'We are your bone and flesh', they said (2 *Samuel* 5:1).

This expression of community solidarity jars on our ears. We can accept it when a married man describes his wife as his 'other half', but few of us think of the Prime Minister in quite the same way. And our concern for less well-off members of society tends to be remote — unless, of course, one of the family happens to be disabled or unemployed.

In the Old Testament covenant community everyone else was 'one of the family'. You supported the bereaved, fed the hungry, and took the immigrant into your home because they were all 'bone of your bone and flesh of your flesh'.

Social concern was as much part of God-centred living in Old Testament times as religious observance. When people tried to drive a wedge between the two, the prophets exposed their hypocrisy in the strongest terms. 'When you spread out your hands in prayer', says God through Isaiah, 'I will hide my eyes from you; even if you offer many prayers, I will not listen. . . .

Stop doing wrong, learn to do right! Seek justice, encourage the oppressed. Defend the cause of the fatherless, plead the case of the widow.' (*Isaiah* 1:15–17). 'Hear this, you who trample the needy and do away with the poor of the land', thunders Amos, 'I will turn your religious feasts into mourning and all your singing into weeping.' (*Amos* 8:4, 10). Splitting community care from worship was like trying to separate heads from tails on a coin. The two belonged together.

**Love your neighbour**

Jesus left his disciples in no doubt about their obligations to the community. He made no secret of the fact that they would attract opposition if they tried to live up to his standards, but they were not to withdraw from society just to escape hurt. Although they were not 'of' the world (in the sense that they were to live distinctively), he deliberately sent them 'into' the world, to make an important impact on it by lives of service (see *John* 17:14–18).

He led the way himself. 'If one of you wants to be great', he said, 'he must be the servant of the rest. For even the Son of Man did not come to be served: he came to serve and to give his life to redeem many people.' (*Mark* 10:43–45; see also *Luke* 22:24–27). So when John the Baptist, sitting depressed and tortured by doubt in a prison cell, sent some of his followers to check up on Jesus' credentials, the answer came back in a catalogue of social service: 'Go back and tell John what you are hearing and seeing: the blind can see, the lame can walk, those who suffer from dreaded skin diseases are made clean, the deaf hear, the dead are brought back to life, and the Good News is preached to the poor.' (*Matthew* 11:2–6).

Jesus' main aim in life was to speak to people's minds and souls, but he never ignored their physical and material needs. His healing miracles demonstrated his concern for men and women as whole people, not simply as souls with ears. And he demanded that his followers shared the same all-round concern and care. Those who called him 'Lord', he warned, but failed to feed the hungry, welcome the stranger, clothe the naked and care for the sick, were in fact rejecting him — as God's Day of Judgement would make plain (see *Matthew* 25:31–46).

Christians have sometimes been accused of caring for people's bodies in order to get at their souls. Fifty years ago, some missionaries were blamed for using food, medicine and education as

The 'meals on wheels' service makes sure that elderly or disabled shut-ins get at least one square meal a day. Is it simply a question of nourishing food, or can you see other advantages?

bait to bring unwilling non-Christians into the church. In other words, their practical concern for others had ulterior motives. This made the great Indian statesman Gandhi protest, 'I hold that proselytizing under the cloak of humanitarian work is, to say the least, unhealthy. Why should I change my religion because a doctor who professes Christianity as his religion has cured me of some disease?'

If some Christians have earned this criticism, they cannot put the blame on Christ. He laid enormous stress on the need for selfless motives in serving others. The way you give, he said, means even more than how much you give (see *Matthew* 6:2–4). Those who offer a service must do so without expecting any kind of return (see *Luke* 6:32–35 and 14:12–14). And once again he led the way himself by personal example. According to the Gospel writers, when he met a crowd of hungry people, or a couple of blind beggars, or a bereaved woman, or a leper, he went to their aid not because he wanted to add to the number of his followers. He simply 'had compassion on them'. (see *Matthew* 14:14, 20:34; *Mark* 1:41; *Luke* 7:13).

Above all, Jesus taught, Christians who serve others should do so in the knowledge that they are following God's own lead. They should show mercy to others because he is merciful (see *Luke* 6:36). They should even show practical love towards their personal enemies, because that is the way God treats those who insult or ignore him, 'for he makes his sun to shine on bad and good people alike, and gives rain to those who do good and to those who do evil.' (*Matthew* 5:43–45).

The rest of the New Testament accurately reflects Jesus' teaching and example. God 'has created us for a life of good deeds', writes Paul (*Ephesians* 2:10). 'Let love make you serve one another. For the whole law is summed up in one commandment: "Love your neighbour as you love yourself." ' (*Galatians* 5:13–14).

The seeds of Christian community care were therefore sown in the very earliest days of the church's life. Christian generosity quickly became proverbial. 'There was no-one in the group who was in need', Luke reports, because 'no-one said that any of his belongings was his own, but they all shared with one another everything they had.' (*Acts* 4:32–35). The whole purpose of earning a wage, adds Paul, is to provide you with even more to give away (see *Ephesians* 4:28). After all, had not Jesus himself said 'There is more happiness in giving than in receiving'? (*Acts* 20:35).

'Christianity is a rebellion against natural law, a protest against nature', wrote Adolf Hitler. 'Taken to its logical extreme, Christianity would mean the systematic cult of human failure.'

In a way, Hitler was right. If 'natural law' means the law of the jungle, the Christian gospel is certainly a protest against it. The whole of the Bible's teaching calls Christians to hunt out and support 'human failures', not to eliminate them so that only the strongest survive. Biblical Christianity has no place for religion without community service. In John's words, 'If anyone has material possessions and sees his brother in need but has no pity on him, how can the love of God be in him?' (*1 John* 3:17).

## Questions for discussion

1. What obligations (if any) have we as individuals to the community?
2. What can an individual gain from taking part in community service?
3. To what extent does the Welfare State meet the needs of the less well-off members of society?
4. What do you think of the idea that some criminals should do community service instead of serving jail sentences?

# 12. Addiction

There are very few people who have never taken a drug of any sort. A cup of coffee or tea contains quite a powerful drug. So, of course, does a cigarette or a pint of beer. And most of us have had a prescription from the doctor at one time or another. The discovery of new and better drugs has brought tremendous benefits to mankind.

Drugs bring their dangers, however, as well as their benefits. Most of them act as selective poisons on the body. We may feel that they give us something extra, but that is really an illusion. What usually happens is that they kill bacterial invaders or suppress the body's warning systems (which makes us feel better); or change the balance of our body chemistry (which makes us feel different).

Many drugs are addictive — that is, they work on the body in such a way that the user, sooner or later, becomes dependent on them. Some cause *physical* dependence. Opiates (such as heroin and morphine) and barbiturates (sedatives, including sleeping pills) are drugs of this kind. So, too, is alcohol. There are more men and women in Britain addicted to alcohol today than there are people addicted to all other drugs put together.

Not everyone who takes one of these drugs is, of course, addicted to it. Much depends on the amount taken. This is why nearly all drugs are only available on prescription, or have their sales restricted in some other way. A lot depends on the individual as well. The effect of any drug will vary a great deal from person to person.

Other drugs create *psychic* dependence. They are not like heroin and barbiturates, as they do not alter body chemistry so greatly that terrible physical withdrawal symptoms follow when the addict attempts to break the habit. However — like heroin and barbiturates — they do induce a strong craving for more. The World Health Organization defines psychic dependence as 'a psychic drive which requires periodic or chronic administration of the substance for pleasure or to avoid discomfort'.

Drugs which cause psychic, but not physical, dependence include cannabis (the effect of which varies widely) and amphetamines (pep pills). Amphetamines make people very lively and talkative for a while, but then often lead to deep depression — which naturally makes the user want another dose for a 'lift'. Psychedelic drugs such as LSD also come in this category. Those on LSD trips have hallucinations and experience a sharpening of their senses (colours, for example, seem much brighter). Unfortunately, horrific side-effects can also occur (such as nightmares and terrible feelings of fear).

The number of drug addicts has risen sharply in the last few years. Apart from alcoholics (at least 300 000 people in Britain have a serious drink problem, according to the Royal College of Psychiatrists), there were 4000 registered addicts in 1981 receiving treatment in clinics and hospitals. And the medical authorities reckon that for every addict who registers, there are about 20 who do not.

## Why do people become addicts?

Most people who take drugs do it for pleasure. They enjoy the feeling, so they get deeper into the habit. And some, without meaning to do so, become addicts.

There are deeper reasons, too, why some people grow dependent on drugs. Here are the three main ones that the psychologists have identified:

(i) *A desire to be accepted.*   In some circles, drug-taking is a status symbol. If you do it, you are 'in'; if you refuse, you are 'out'. Most people want to belong to some group, so the pressures to conform are very strong. We see it in styles of dress and in musical tastes. If your friends smoke pot at parties, it is as hard to be the odd one out as it would be to turn up at a disco in a city suit with a Beethoven sonata under your arm.

Most alcoholics started out as social drinkers. William Booth, founder of the Salvation Army, recognized this. 'Many a man takes to beer', he wrote, 'not from the love of beer, but from a natural craving for the light, warmth, company and comfort which is thrown in along with the beer, and which he cannot get except by buying beer.'

(ii) *A desire to escape.*   This can take various forms. Some people take to drugs as an escape from boredom. Their lives seem tedious and drab. They find no satisfaction in sport or music, so they turn to drugs as a source of excitement. Others use drug-taking as an escape-route from their environment. They long to opt out of the rat-race, but cannot. 'Trips' are their way of protesting against the bankruptcy (as they see it) of the society that enslaves them. It is their path to freedom.

Others again have deeply personal problems from which they feel a desperate need to escape. A drug such as heroin can temporarily obliterate worry, so the drug becomes a kind of a crutch. The addict prefers his or her own private world of phantasy to the real world of helplessness and strain. Sometimes 'prefers' is the wrong word, and drug-taking is a thinly disguised cry for help. As one addict put it, 'I used to want help but I couldn't say so. I only got it when I became a junkie.'

(iii) *A desire for spiritual experience.*   In 1963 Dr Timothy Leary was dismissed from his Harvard University teaching post in the U.S.A. for encouraging hundreds of student volunteers to experiment with LSD and other psychedelic drugs. He said at the time, 'If you are serious about your religion, if you really wish to commit yourself to the spiritual quest, you must learn how to use psychochemicals. Drugs are the religion of the twenty-first century.'

Despite the note of novelty in those words, the use of drugs as a spiritual aid is nothing new. As Leary knew very well, Eastern religions have used cannabis in this way for centuries. That is why Zen Buddhism and 'Krishna consciousness' have become so popular on the underground drug scene.

Some people use drugs as an alternative to prayer and meditation. They look upon LSD not as a way out of real life, but as a way into intense mystical experiences which will lift them beyond the humdrum body-bound routine of ordinary daily living.

**The Christian view**

The Christian church is very firmly against the use of drugs to the point of addiction. There are positive reasons for this negative reaction, as we shall see. In particular, the Christian gospel has definitions of *pleasure*, *freedom* and *spirituality* which are incompatible with drug dependence.

(i) *Pleasure.* Some people believe that Christians are against drugs because they are against pleasure of all kinds. But this is far from the truth. A glance at the Bible's attitude to alcohol is enough to dispel any false impressions of that sort.

Wine was part of Israel's staple diet, and a source of great satisfaction and happiness, especially at times of celebration. 'You make grass grow for the cattle and plants for man to use', sings the Psalmist, 'and you produce wine to make him happy' (*Psalms* 104:14–15), 'Drink your wine and be cheerful', Ecclesiastes adds, 'feasting makes you happy and wine cheers you up.' (*Ecclesiastes* 9:7, 10:19).

Right down to the present day, the Jewish community has treated alcohol as a gift of God. Every major Jewish festival is marked by the drinking of wine. Even young children are given small cupfuls on sabbaths and at festival time. And yet in any table of alcohol statistics you will find the Jews right at the bottom of the list, if they feature there at all.

Jesus showed the same positive approach. He was glad to join in the wedding celebrations at Cana, and he provided more wine (600 litres of it!) when supplies ran out (see *John* 2:1–10). He entered into social life so freely that he was criticized by the kill-joys of the time as 'a glutton and a drunkard' (see *Matthew* 11:19). And, on a different note altogether, he commanded his disciples to break bread and drink wine as a lasting reminder of the meaning of his death (see *Matthew* 26:26–29 and *1 Corinthians* 11:23–25).

Christianity is far from being against pleasure. Nevertheless, it does define pleasure in a special way. In particular, it insists that *genuine personal enjoyment puts other people's interests first*. Jesus himself taught that complete joy comes only to those who love others in practical ways (see *John* 15:10–12). Later, Paul repeats some other words of Jesus which strike the same note: 'the Lord Jesus himself said, "There is more happiness in giving than in receiving".' (*Acts* 20:35).

Putting the same thing the other way round, selfish enjoyment is by definition false pleasure, from a Christian point of view. The man who offers a drink to an alcoholic is not sharing his enjoyment. He is putting the other person at great risk. 'The right thing to do', comments Paul again, 'is to keep from eating meat, drinking wine or doing anything else that will make your brother fall.' (*Romans* 14:21).

This is a major reason why Christianity will always fight

addiction. The addicts' pleasure is self-centred and often selfish. Their habit erects barriers between themselves and other people. A drunk may sing his head off, but he does not communicate, let alone consider others. Sometimes his addiction may make him a threat. In December 1979, the Chairman of the Parole Board said that alcohol was a significant factor in half of all murders and crimes of unpremeditated violence.

(ii) *Freedom*.   Addicts may take drugs to break free from themselves and their environment. But all they have done, as Christians see it, is to crawl out of one prison cell into another. The moment they lose control of their mind or body, they become slaves to a habit.

The Bible sets a high value on self-control. It is part of the Holy Spirit's fruit in the believer's life (see *Galatians* 5:22–23). And the one thing a drunk or drugged person does not have is control of self. The Book of Proverbs' description of a hangover paints an amusing but penetrating picture of the drunk's 'freedom': 'Don't let wine tempt you, even though it is rich red, though it sparkles in the cup, and it goes down smoothly. The next morning you will feel as if you had been bitten by a poisonous snake. Weird sights will appear before your eyes, and you will not be able to think or speak clearly. You will feel as though you were out on the ocean, sea-sick, swinging high up in the rigging of a tossing ship. "I must have been hit", you will say; "I must have been beaten up, but I don't remember it. Why can't I wake up? I need another drink." ' (*Proverbs* 23:31–35).

To those who want to escape from life, the Christian gospel offers hope and 'life in all its fulness', as Jesus described it (*John* 10:10). It distinguishes sharply between escapism, and freedom to face reality with confidence and expectancy. Aldous Huxley took a psychedelic drug when he was told he was dying. Jesus was offered drugged wine on the way to the cross, but he refused it (see *Matthew* 27:34).

(iii) *Spirituality*.   People who take psychedelic drugs certainly have 'out of the body' experiences which are very similar to those described by religious mystics. Both appear to stimulate the same area of the brain. But the two kinds of experience are in fact quite different. One Indian mystic who investigated psychedelic 'trips' summed up his findings like this: 'The (LSD) experience is as far removed from reality as a mirage from water. No matter how much one pursues the mirage, one will never reach water, and the search for God through drugs must end in disillusionment.'

From the Christian point of view, the criticism can be sharpened in two ways. In the first place, Christian spiritual experience is meant to equip the believer to deal more effectively with life's challenges. The drug experience, by contrast, is an escape from real life, deliberately intended to be irrelevant to it.

Secondly, the Christian life is about character, not sensation. The 'tripper' aims solely for a beautiful experience. For the Christian, such experience — if it comes — is incidental, not central. Hugh Montefiore, Bishop of Birmingham, painted the contrast this way in writing about the drug scene of the early 1970s: 'Contrast the Beat Gospel with the Gospel Beatitudes. The beats say: "Happy are those who take a trip. Happy are those who find ecstatic illusions. Happy are those who contract out of the world." But Jesus said in the original Beatitudes: "Happy are the meek, the humble, the pure in heart, those who hunger and thirst after righteousness . . ." '

All Christians would agree with the contrast the Bishop is drawing, but some would feel that at least one more thing needs to be said. To most addicts, the church stands for everything they want to escape from — complacency, half-heartedness and compromise. Church leaders can only expect drug addicts to listen to what they say, when they demonstrate effectively that they have a more satisfying alternative to offer.

## Questions for discussion

1. Why do you think the number of alcoholics is rising?
2. How far can taking drugs answer people's problems?
3. What do you think of the Christian definitions of pleasure, freedom and spirituality?
4. What would be the advantages and disadvantages of legalizing pot?

# 13. Race and colour

People move around the world much faster today than ever before. Businessmen jet across continents to discuss their deals. Holidaymakers travel overseas on package tours. And even those of us who stay at home find that the other side of the globe is as near as our television sets. Evening by evening, news programmes and feature films introduce us to faraway places and to the interesting people who live there.

Unfortunately, the picture is not a completely rosy one. It seems that whenever people from different racial backgrounds meet at close quarters for any length of time, there is conflict. Apparently, it is one thing to visit a foreign country for a fortnight's holiday or to go out to a Chinese restaurant for an evening meal, but it is altogether different to have a family of immigrants move in next door, or to find that your sister is going out with a boy whose skin is a different colour. And so, on a larger scale, our T.V. screens are filled with news of race riots, anti-apartheid demonstrations and all the other signs of racial prejudice and discrimination.

Why should this be? The reasons go deep into human nature, but the root cause is fear. We suspect strangers mainly because we feel that they threaten our way of life. We are afraid of the changes and competition they may bring with them. The sociologists talk about a 'toleration level' in any community. When one or two immigrant families move into a neighbourhood, they are tolerated, even if they are not welcomed. But if the streets fill up with newcomers, tolerance quickly changes to resentment and hostility. The local residents fear for their jobs. They object strongly to changes they see in their shops and schools. And the seeds of conflict are quickly sown.

Many different ways have been suggested of solving the problems resulting from immigration. We shall look at the four main ones, before going on to consider the special contribution Christianity can make to the issue of racism in general.

### Attitudes to immigrants

Two extreme 'solutions' have been put forward. They sound like opposites, but they really have the same aim — to reduce the impact a group of immigrants are likely to have on the host community.

(i) *Exclude them.* In the United Kingdom, this extreme view is associated with the name of the Ulster M.P., Enoch Powell. In his opinion, immigrants are an 'alien wedge' in society. Their numbers should therefore be reduced (by encouraging them to go back home) and all future immigration should be stopped.

This apparently simple solution begs an enormous number of questions. Is this attitude based on colour prejudice? Should we, for example, ban all white immigrants as well as coloured ones?

European immigrants into Britain regularly outnumber those from the West Indies and Asia put together. And if we are to focus on colour alone, where do black teenagers born and bred in Liverpool or Bradford go, if they are supposed to go 'home'?

Nevertheless, such opinions command wide support. After one powerful speech Enoch Powell received 100 000 letters, more than 99 per cent of them agreeing with him. He had predicted 'rivers of blood' if immigration was allowed to continue. And this points us to the main plank in the political platform of all those who want to exclude immigrants, whether from Britain or elsewhere. People of different races, they say, will never live together in peace. So, to avoid conflict, they must be kept apart — just as the best way to stop fights in school playgrounds is to separate those who would otherwise start them.

(ii) *Absorb them.* At the other extreme stand those who welcome immigrants, provided they adapt themselves completely to the community they join. Sikh men who ride motor-bikes must wear crash-helmets like everyone else, despite their turbans, even if it cuts across their culture to do so. Children from Islamic or Jewish homes must forget their religious scruples about food when they eat school dinners, and not expect special menus to be provided for them. Right down to details of dress and hairstyle, it is argued, the outsiders must do all that is humanly possible to become just like the insiders.

Some immigrants are more willing than others to be 'absorbed' in this way. English-speaking West Indians from a Christian background, for example, generally find it easier to adapt than Asians who make a big effort to guard their distinctive religions, dress, languages and diet. Those who argue for absorption point to the dangers of hanging on jealously to these cultural differences. It only makes for resentment, they say. Who can really blame the English parent who complained 'My son is one of only four white children in his class. They have an Indian teacher and are learning more about Indian customs than the English way of life.'?

In between these extremes come two other viewpoints. These apply to all societies with racial minorities, and not just to host communities receiving immigrants.

(iii) *Segregate them.*   This is really the apartheid principle, practised most obviously in South Africa. Its supporters do not want to *exclude* any racial group, but they do want to keep all racial groups *apart* — right down to separate park seats, and separate ambulances to take patients to different hospital wards. Mixed marriages, of course, are strictly banned.

Those who favour apartheid argue that they are only using the letter of the law to enforce ordinary people's natural inclination to keep themselves to themselves. As one very experienced traveller put it, 'It is a pity that the Afrikaans word for separate and equal development is precisely what black people everywhere most desire — in North America, in Britain, or in Africa.'

Unfortunately, that is a very one-sided view of the way a segregation policy operates. Although apartheid means 'separation and equality', it does not work out that way at all. In practice, some are always more equal than others. In South Africa, even the division of land is grossly unequal. The black Africans, who make up 67 per cent of the population, are allocated only 13 per cent of the territory. Lord Brockway was much nearer the truth when he wrote, 'apartheid means continuous and comprehensive humiliation of all non-whites'.

(iv) *Integrate them.*   Roy Jenkins, when he was British Home Secretary, defined this fourth approach as 'not a flattening process of assimilation, but equal opportunity accompanied by cultural diversity in an atmosphere of mutual tolerance'. In other words, a policy of integration in a racially mixed community will ensure justice for all. It will also promote harmony by encouraging different groups to build bridges of understanding between one another.

Integrating minority groups is not the same as absorbing them. The difference is like that between stirring sugar into a cup of coffee and building a brick into a wall. The sugar is 'absorbed' into a cup of coffee, losing its identity. The brick is 'integrated' in the wall, remaining distinctive but closely bonded to all the other bricks. When immigrants are *absorbed* into a community, they lose all their distinctive customs and culture, but when they are fully *integrated*, they keep their cultural distinctiveness and share its richness with everyone else.

## A Christian approach

Against this background it becomes easier to appreciate the special contribution Christian teaching can make to racial problems. There was apparently no colour bar in biblical times, but racial conflicts were certainly known — especially between Jews and non-Jews.

(i) *Equality in creation.* Christianity shares this first conviction with the Jewish faith. 'When God created man', declares the book of Genesis, 'he made him in the likeness of God.' (*Genesis 5:1*). Before their Creator, in other words, all people are absolutely equal in status. As one ancient piece of Jewish literature quaintly puts it, no-one can claim 'I am descended from a more distinguished Adam than you!'

The apostle Paul seized upon this point when he was teaching in the Greek city of Athens. 'From one man', he told his non-Jewish audience, 'God created all races of mankind.' (*Acts* 17:26). And the apostle Peter, who was very much a Jewish racist at heart, had already been driven to the same conclusion. 'I now realize', he said, 'that it is true that God treats everyone on the same basis. Whoever worships him and does what is right is acceptable to him, no matter what race he belongs to.' (*Acts* 10:34–35).

In practical terms, this means that Christians must fight racial discrimination wherever they find it. The God of the Bible is passionately concerned for social justice. To quote the Old Testament again, 'For all time to come, the same rules are binding on you and on the foreigners who live among you. You and they are alike in the Lord's sight. ' (*Numbers* 15:15). It is a clear Christ-

ian duty, therefore, to protest loudly whenever one person is
treated less favourably than another on grounds of colour, race
or national origin (which is how the British law defines
discrimination).

Exactly the same guidelines apply in judging attitudes which,
though perfectly legal, suggest that one racial group is inferior to
another in any way. Such attitudes can even creep into our most
respectable books used in schools. One West Indian girl, for
example, tells how she felt 'wordless and numb inside' when she
read in her school library's copy of *The Encylopaedia Britannica*:
'The negro would appear to stand on a lower evolutionary plane
than the white man, and to be more closely related to the highest
anthropoids.' Fortunately, that article has since been re-written.
Check the copy in *your* library!

(ii) *Reconciliation in Christ.*   The law can go a long way towards
putting an end to *discrimination*, but it is powerless to change
*prejudice*. The difference is important. Discrimination is to do with
actions and words, but prejudice is a matter of the mind and
heart. The law can force a prejudiced employer to take on coloured people alongside whites in his labour force, but it cannot
make him love or like them any the more.

Jesus went one step further than the law in this respect. He
taught '*love* your neighbour as yourself', and explained what he
meant by telling a racist story (*Luke* 10:26–37). The Samaritan
passer-by would have been quite within the law to ignore the
bleeding Jew in the gutter, and walk on with a prejudiced sneer.
Instead of that, he went out of his way to give him first aid. And
Jesus' punch-line was a challenge to all who believe in exclusion
or segregation: 'Go and do likewise.'

The New Testament sees the life and death of Jesus as a
bridge which brings divided groups of people together. Writing
about the deepest racial split he knew (the rift between Jews and
non-Jews), Paul put it like this: 'For Christ himself has brought
us peace by making Jews and non-Jews one people. With his
own body he broke down the wall that separated them and kept
them enemies . . . in order to create out of the two races one new
people in union with himself, in this way making peace. By his
death on the cross Christ destroyed their enmity; by means of
the cross he united both races into one body and brought them
back to God.' (*Ephesians* 2:14–16).

This reconciliation that the New Testament teaches is not the colourless kind of harmony that comes about when one racial group is absorbed into another. It is much more like the integrated brick in the wall than the spoonful of sugar that is lost in the cup of coffee. Paul himself made that plain when he said 'There is neither Jew nor Greek' and — in the same breath — '*male nor female*', before he concluded 'for you are all one in Christ Jesus.' (*Galatians* 3:28). A relationship between a man and a woman becomes closer when they share their differences, not when they ignore them. And the same is true of relationships between people of different races.

In his autobiography, the Black Power leader Malcolm X wrote: 'Christianity is the white man's religion. The Holy Bible in the white man's hands and his interpretations of it have been the greatest single ideological weapon for enslaving millions of non-white human beings.' Unfortunately, some Christians are not faithful to the example of Christ. He lived and died to bridge all racial divisions created by people. A former Archbishop of Cape Town summed it up like this: 'My fellow-man's relationship to God is equivalent to mine. What I am in the sight of God, so is he.'

## Questions for discussion

1. Why is there conflict when people from different racial backgrounds mix?
2. How justified are some people's prejudices?
3. Which of the four 'solutions' to the racial problems, listed in this chapter, do you favour?
4. Is it right to force groups of people to live together when they do not want to?

# 14. Crime and punishment

Punishment is meant to hurt. There is no getting away from that. A caning hurts physically. A fine hurts financially. A prison sentence, like an hour's detention, hurts you by robbing you of your freedom. If a punishment does not hurt at all, it loses its point.

And that causes problems for Christians, because Jesus taught so often that hurting people is wrong. He told his followers not to take revenge on others in a 'tit for tat' kind of way. 'If anyone slaps you on the right cheek', he said, 'let him slap your left cheek too.' (*Matthew* 5:38–39; compare that with *Romans* 12:17–21, where Paul says much the same thing.) Peter once asked how many times a person should suffer injustice before hitting back. Seven times, perhaps? 'No, not seven times', Jesus answered, 'but seventy times seven' — which was his way of saying, 'Keep forgiving, and stop counting!' (*Matthew* 18:21–22).

Strong words like those suggest that Christians ought really to be campaigning for the abolition of all punishment. But that would mean taking a very one-sided view of Jesus' teaching. He was not, in fact, at all soft or sentimental when he came across wrongdoing. He often spoke out in support of justice. He even warned about 'eternal punishment' for those who lived selfish lives (see *Matthew* 25:41–46). It sometimes surprises readers of the New Testament Gospels to discover that Jesus taught more about God's punishment in the after-life than any other person in the Bible (see, for example, *Matthew* 10:28, 12:36–37 and *John* 5:24–29).

So we must include this sterner aspect in our view of punishment, if we want to find a genuinely Christian balance. Otherwise we risk being more 'Christian' than Christ himself.

One way of putting the pieces of the puzzle together is to ask the question, '*Why* punish offenders?' Three different answers can be given.

(i) *To pay them back*. This is sometimes known as the principle of retribution. If a person does something wrong, he or she must pay the appropriate penalty. In other words, the punishment must always fit the crime.

There is something very attractive about this rough and ready method of administering justice. Everyone knows exactly where he or she is, especially the offender. There is no question of 'getting off' if the jury finds him or her guilty. All the judge or magistrates have to do is to look up the crime in the index of their law books and read out the fixed sentence.

Prisoners themselves recognize the fairness of this approach. They know they are getting exactly what their crime deserves — nothing more and nothing less. As one of the crucified men next to Jesus put it, 'Our sentence is only right, because we are getting what we deserve for what we did: but he has done no wrong.' (*Luke* 23:41). Sometimes convicted people may even resent it when they receive too light a sentence. One famous lawyer tells how, in the days before capital punishment was abolished, some murderers he defended were quite angry when they were reprieved.

The principle of retribution is, in fact, one of the main arguments used by those who want to bring back (or keep) the death penalty for murder. If you take another person's life, it seems obviously right that you should forfeit your own. The Old Testament certainly supports that point of view. 'Whoever sheds the blood of man', says the book of *Genesis* (9:6), 'by man shall his blood be shed'. Indeed, the idea of making the punishment fit the crime (for everything, not just murder) finds a great deal of support in the New Testament as well as the Old. Paul puts it very simply in *Galatians* 6:7: 'A person will reap exactly what he sows.' And, he adds, God himself will judge everyone by this standard one day: 'For all of us must appear before Christ, to be judged by him. Each one will receive what he deserves . . .' (*2 Corinthians* 5:10).

Some people object that 'paying back' an offender is an un-Christian idea, because it does what Jesus forbade. Punishing people in this way, they argue, is really just the primitive urge to take revenge, dressed up in a judge's wig to make it look respectable. But that is not really a valid objection. There is all the difference in the world between hitting back when you are hurt (which Jesus certainly ruled out) and demanding the punishment of those who hurt *others*. A law-court never allows the victim to punish the offender.

There is, however, one very serious drawback in an approach to punishment which focuses only on retribution. And this takes us on to the second answer that can be given to our question, '*Why* punish offenders?'

(ii) *To reform them.*   If we insist that the punishment must always fit the offence, we may end up by being unfair to the offender. Take, for example, two drivers who go over the speed limit. One has had too much to drink and is determined to beat everyone else to the next set of traffic lights for the sheer fun of it. The other is getting a sick neighbour to hospital as fast as she can, to get him urgent medical help. It would obviously be quite wrong to punish those two people in identical ways simply because they have committed the same offence.

When we punish, therefore — some would say — our eyes should be on the offenders, not on what they have done. Our aim should be to help and heal them, not to pay them back.

Jesus certainly reacted to wrong-doers in this way. When a woman was brought to him who had been caught in the act of committing adultery, he was far more interested in her future welfare (and in the motives of those who had brought her!) than he was in the law's fixed penalty for her offence (*John* 8:3–11). And the whole point behind his famous parable of the lost son (*Luke* 15:11–32) was to show how the father in the story treated his tearaway son in a way he certainly did not deserve.

Seen in this light, some of our traditional methods of punishment can be seriously challenged. Prison, for example, rarely does very much to reform those who are sent there. It blurs their sense of responsibility for what they have done, by isolating them from the people they have hurt. It often acts as a 'school for criminals' by arming them with new and better ideas to make crime pay. And it nearly always makes it harder for them to find a job when they get out.

For all these reasons, alternatives to imprisonment are being suggested, such as compulsory community service, which may not sound nearly so severe, but which may do far more in the long run to reform offenders. It is interesting that in Old Testament times a thief had to pay compensation to those he robbed and a mugger had to pay for his victim's medical expenses and lost wages. A modern prison sentence makes both those things impossible.

Nevertheless, just as with the principle of retribution, there are big problems with a view of punishment that sees its *only* purpose as to reform offenders. It seems unfair, for example, to punish one person lightly and another severely when they have committed the same crime — even if it can be proved that the one would benefit from a prison sentence, while the other would be harmed by it.

Confusion is created in the mind of the general public, too. As one bewildered mother commented, when her daughter's murderer was sentenced to three years' imprisonment, 'Is that all my little girl's life is worth?' Such a light penalty might have been the very best way to reform that particular offender, but the impression left in the mother's mind was that today's courts do not think killing children is as serious as robbing banks.

And that leads us on to the third answer to our question. *Why* punish offenders? The main purpose, some would say, is:

(iii) *To deter them.* The general public needs protection from social menaces. Crime is like a disease, the argument goes, and the purpose of punishment is to stop the disease spreading. Criminals must be punished so severely that they will think twice before committing the same offence again. And those who read about their fate in the newspapers will be put off from attempting the same thing themselves.

The idea of crime being a threat to society's health is one that the Bible often uses in its teaching about punishment. 'In this way you will remove this evil', says the Old Testament in defending the use of the death penalty. 'Then everyone will hear of it and be afraid, and no-one else will dare to act in such a way.' (*Deuteronomy* 17:7, 13)

The general public needs *educating*, too. As Lord Chief Justice Denning put it, 'The ultimate justification of punishment is the emphatic denunciation of a crime.' In other words, people's ideas about right and wrong are weakened or reinforced by the way the courts punish offenders. If those who smash telephone boxes are severely punished, the idea will soon get around that this is a serious offence that the community will not tolerate. But if they are let off with a caution, the impression will grow that vandalism does not really matter.

Unfortunately, treating punishment as *just* a deterrent can have very bad consequences. In particular, society's interests may swamp the rights of the individual. It may be very tempting, for example, to try to stamp out football hooliganism by giving long prison sentences to the few who are caught — even though such a severe punishment is quite unfair to the individuals concerned. An occasion could even arise when society would gain great benefits from the punishment of a totally innocent person. One community leader defended the execution of Jesus on these grounds. 'Don't you realize', he argued, 'that it is better for you to let one man die for the people, instead of having the whole nation destroyed?' (*John* 11:50).

*Why* punish offenders? We have found three answers to our question. The first focused our attention on the offence, the second on the offender, and the third on society.

We have also discovered that none of these answers, taken on its own, is completely adequate. If we insist on making the punishment fit the crime, we run the risk of treating some offenders too harshly. If we shut our eyes to everything but the need to reform the offender, we end up by treating some offences too leniently. And if we always put society's interests first, deterrence may mask injustice to the individual.

The solution, of course, is to keep our eyes on all three aspects at once — the offence, the offender and the needs of society. That is certainly what the Bible encourages us to do. It will not always be easy to strike the right balance. How, for example, should a shoplifter be punished? Should he be fined five times the price of the stolen article, as a punishment to match his crime? Should he be jailed, to protect other shoppers and deter other thieves? Or should he be sent to hospital to 'dry out', if it turns out that he is an alcoholic who has stolen a bottle of whisky?

The answers may sometimes be difficult, but the questions must always be asked, if we are to approach the problem of crime and punishment in a genuinely Christian way.

## Questions for discussion

1. What should be the aim of punishment?
2. What are the difficulties in having one unalterable penalty for each crime?

*How should offenders be treated? Life in a maximum security block (above) must seem like being a caged animal in a zoo. Does the punishment do any good? What might be the views of mugged P. C. Ian Bennett (below)?*

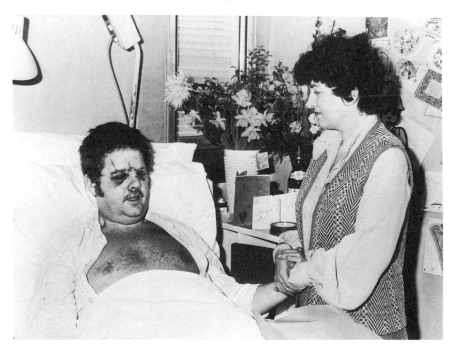

3. Do prison sentences act as a deterrent, or do they just aggravate problems? What alternatives to imprisonment do you prefer?
4. Do you think capital punishment should be brought back?

# 15.  Unwanted life

Most people are glad to be alive, but not all life is wanted. The girl who gets pregnant nine months before important exams would willingly get rid of the life in her womb. And the old man with incurable cancer, and nothing to live for, would welcome death with dignity.

Abortion and euthanasia offer answers to these problems. There is nothing new about either. The history books tell us that drugs have always been available (though often illegally) to end unwanted life.

Nevertheless, modern medicine has made many of these problems even more acute. Down's Syndrome, for example, can now be diagnosed before birth — but that only adds to the moral pressures both doctors and parents face in deciding whether or not to end a pregnancy which may result in the birth of a deformed baby. And at the other end of life, medical technology has advanced so far that patients can now be kept clinically alive for years, even though it is extremely doubtful whether their lives are worth living. Progress has simply made it more difficult to decide when the patient should be allowed to die.

Traditionally, Christians have been against both euthanasia and abortion. To find out why, we need to probe Christian teaching about both *life* and *love*.

## Life

Medical progress has raised difficult questions about the nature of life. Our attitudes to abortion and euthanasia will very much depend on the answers we accept.

(i) *When does human life begin?*  If the fetus in the womb is a real person, with full human rights from the moment of conception, abortion has to be put in the same category as homicide. There is then no real moral difference between terminating a pregnancy and killing a baby. If, on the other hand, life only begins at birth, the fetus is an 'it', not a 'he' or a 'she', until its day of birth. Abortion can then be seen as just an extension of contraception.

It is obviously vital to know which view to take of life before birth. Unfortunately, the doctors cannot really help us here. They can, of course, prove that the fetus is physically alive, but they cannot tell us whether or not human personality begins in the womb. That is a moral question, not a physical one.

Advances in technology (especially the use of sonar scanners and fibre optics to take pictures of the fetus in the womb) are certainly making it more and more difficult to see a sharp distinction between the nature of life before and after birth. The old, popular view that getting rid of a fetus is no more immoral than getting rid of a nagging appendix is now seriously outdated.

New discoveries in ante-natal medicine have made some specialists change their minds completely on the morality of abortion. Dr Bernard Nathanson, for example, an American obstetrician who used to campaign strongly for abortion on demand, is now openly against abortion as a result of his clinical research. 'I became acutely aware', he says, 'that this is a patient. This, the fetus, is a person. It is not a lump of meat. What we see is us. It is not a tadpole swimming around. It is a part of our community. It listens, it hears, it behaves like us.'

It has long been a strongly-held Christian belief that human personality begins before birth. The Roman Catholic church's stand on this issue is particularly well known. 'Abortion has been considered homicide since the first centuries of the Church', said the Pope in 1970, 'and nothing permits it to be considered otherwise today.'

The Bible assumes rather than teaches this principle. Luke, for example, describes how John the Baptist (still a fetus) leapt for joy when Mary (who had recently become pregnant with Jesus) came to visit his mother. And in the Old Testament, God tells Jeremiah, 'Before I formed you in the womb, I knew you' (*Luke* 1:39–41; *Jeremiah* 1:5). In both cases, the unborn child's personality is taken for granted. The same assumption colours the famous, poetical description of the beginning of life in Psalm 139: 'For you created my unformed body. All the days ordained for me were written in your book before one of them came to be.' (verses 13–16).

(ii) *When does human life end?*   If our stance on abortion depends

very much on our understanding of life before birth, our approach to euthanasia will be strongly influenced by our views on
the end of life. Here, the medical experts invite us to revise the
way death has traditionally been defined.

Until recently, it was generally accepted that a person could
only be certified as dead when his or her heart had stopped
beating. Today, however, life-support machinery can keep the
heart going — even when there is no sign of life in the patient's
brain. That is why doctors now talk in terms of brain death.
When it is clear beyond all doubt that the brain has died, the
respirator is switched off and the heart stops.

From the moral point of view, it is important to see that this
is not euthanasia. 'Pulling the plugs' does not kill the patient in
these cases. It simply recognizes that he or she has already died.

Similarly, it is not really right to talk about euthanasia when
a doctor stops treating terminally ill patients with life-saving
drugs, or gives them such high doses of pain-killers that their life
is endangered. Prolonging life is only one of doctors' moral duties. Their main responsibility towards dying patients is not to
keep them going as long as they can, but to make the life that
remains as pain-free and as comfortable as possible.

Christians have no moral difficulties with either of these
things. As Pope Paul VI put it, 'The duty of the physician consists
more in striving to relieve pain than in prolonging as long as
possible with every available means a life that is *no longer fully
human* and that is naturally coming to its conclusion.'

(iii) *How do you measure life's value?*   I have put the Pope's words
at the end of the last paragraph in italics, because they raise a
particularly acute moral issue. Can a person who is still physically
alive ever be described as 'no longer fully human'? And if so, can
euthanasia (and abortion, in the case of an unborn child) be
justified, on the grounds that the 'life' that is taken is without
any human value?

These questions arise most often in the case of unconscious
patients whose brains show tiny signs of life, but who (in the
doctors' opinion) will never lead more than a cabbage-like exist-
ence. Many of those who favour voluntary euthanasia would
want to go further than that, however. It is seriously suggested
by some that people who suffer from severely disabling diseases
such as quadriplegia and multiple sclerosis should be offered an
end to their lives, as well as the senile and those with chronic

psychiatric disease. Similarly, pro-abortionists would argue that a pregnancy should be terminated automatically if Down's Syndrome, spina bifida or any other serious defect is diagnosed in the fetus.

Most Christians find this line of argument highly dangerous. Dr Margaret White, for example, writes in a Mothers' Union pamphlet that aborting a fetus for possible abnormalities 'breaches an important principle by suggesting that the deaf, the blind and the maimed are disposable.' That principle certainly has deep roots in the Bible, which has plenty to say about the severely handicapped. It encourages the healthy to treat the sick with special care and respect as extra-valuable members of society, not to put them painlessly out of their misery.

Jesus himself set a great value on the lives of sick and handicapped people. He challenged the attitude which regards the severely disabled as disposable, comparing himself to a shepherd who leaves his whole flock to hunt for just one lost animal (*Matthew* 18:12–13).

The basis for this insistence on the value of the individual's life (however valueless he or she may seem) lies in Christians' belief that every man or woman is created in God's image (see, for example, *Genesis* 5:1–2 and *James* 3:8–9). That fact alone sets human life on a completely different level to animal life, as Jesus clearly taught in *Matthew* 12:12 and *Luke* 12:6. The extra dimension it adds to the lives of human beings makes mercy killing entirely different from putting a sick animal to sleep at the vet's.

## Love

If the Christian approach to *life* loads the scales against abortion and euthanasia, Christ's teaching on *love* seems to tip the balance the other way. Again and again the Gospel writers tell how Jesus was 'filled with pity' for the 'worried and helpless' (*Matthew* 9:36; compare *Matthew* 14:14; *Mark* 1:41 and *Luke* 7:13). Behind every request for abortion or euthanasia there is someone sunk in the depths of worry and helplessness. Would not Jesus want to meet their need by providing facilities for terminating unwanted pregnancies and exhausted lives?

The answer is not quite as easy as it may seem. Loving someone is not the same as doing everything he or she asks. Jesus, in fact, angered many people by refusing to do what they wanted.

Using his teaching as a guideline, there are three tests worth applying to any action which claims to be motivated by love.

(i) *Is it genuinely loving?* Jesus never accepted an apparently loving act at its face value. He knew that compassion could be like a coat of paint on a rusty car, hiding ugly, mixed motives behind a loving veneer. He exposed the hypocrisy, for example, of those who gave to charity only in order to advertise their own generosity (*Matthew* 6:1–4).

All kinds of reasons lie behind appeals for abortion and euthanasia. The mother who advises her teenage girl to end her pregnancy may, in her heart of hearts, be more worried about the harm an illegitimate baby might do to the family's reputation, than genuinely concerned for her daughter's well-being. An apparently compassionate request for euthanasia may mask the revulsion of relatives who feel they cannot cope any more with a long illness. Motives can be terribly mixed. A Scottish doctor tells of a visit he paid to a very sick patient. As he came down the stairs from the patient's bedroom, the relatives surged forward demanding, 'When is this agony going to end?' He looked at them coolly and asked, 'Whose agony?'

(ii) *Does it get to the root of the problem?* Mark tells about a meeting between Jesus and a rich community leader. 'Jesus looked straight at him with love', he reports, 'and said, "Go and sell all you have and give the money to the poor" ' (*Mark* 10:21). When the man turned away in disappointment, Jesus did not lower his demand. To have done so might have seemed loving, but it would not have got to the roots of the problem.

Doctors who specialize in gynaecology and terminal care know that requests for abortion and euthanasia often conceal deeper needs. Many requests for euthanasia, writes Cicely Saunders, medical director of St Christopher's Hospice, 'are cries for help, for the relief of pain and other distress. Once these people have been given welcome and relief, they are glad to be alive.' Rex Gardner, consultant gynaecologist, writes in much the same way about the below-the-surface problems of unmarried women who come to him for abortion. 'To abort a pregnancy because it is extra-marital', he concludes, 'may sound compassionate, but if it does nothing about the underlying problem it has no resemblance to true compassion.'

(iii) *Does it take everyone into consideration?*   Jesus told his famous parables about the Good Samaritan and the Prodigal Son to show his listeners how far genuine compassion must go. In both stories, love embraced people who would normally have been passed over or rejected.

Arguments in favour of abortion and euthanasia can range very widely indeed. *Family* considerations, for example, often weigh heavily. The birth of an unwanted baby can strain family relationships to breaking point. So can the prolonged nursing of a dying relative. *Society's* needs are often brought in, too. With the world's population growing at an alarming rate, why should precious resources be spent on babies who are not wanted and on older people who want to die anyway?

The needs of family and society must certainly be considered, if love is to be as all-embracing as Jesus taught it should be. Nevertheless, there is still another group of people who deserve consideration if the demands of love are to be fully met — the *medical staff* who have the responsibility for carrying out the mercy killing. Their needs and feelings are particularly important from a Christian point of view, because the Bible insists that people must never be used, against their will, as tools to gain other people's goals.

Most doctors would not want to be involved in mercy killing. 'Who is to be the executioner?', asks one G.P. 'The patient's doctor? The nurse? Some other doctor? A technician? Medicine and nursing are caring professions, not killing professions.' The Abortion Act has an exemption clause for doctors and nurses who have conscientious objections, but very few of those who have tested it have found that it works satisfactorily. Many feel very bitter about the burden placed on them by the law as it stands.

Most Christians conclude that abortion and euthanasia are bad solutions to genuine problems. Are there better alternatives? In the case of terminal illness, the solution is already at hand, in the hospice style of care pioneered by Dr Cicely Saunders. All the evidence suggests that appeals for mercy killing will subside if this type of terminal care, which is highly successful in controlling pain and distress, is adopted more widely.

Alternatives to abortion are not so easily found. Organizations such as Life are pioneering the way for women who would be willing to have their babies if they could be sure of adequate

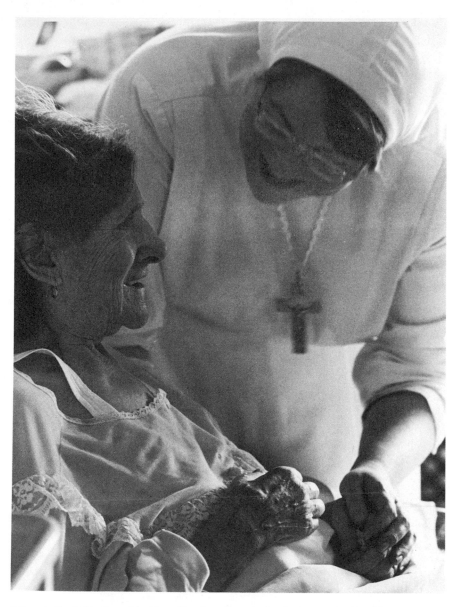

The staff of St. Joseph's Hospice, London, help their terminally ill patients to face up to death with dignity and hope. Compare this approach with the other approach, often found in the past, of not letting patients know they were going to die. Discuss the effects on the patient and the family.

support, but for many that support is not yet available. Many Christians would therefore take the view that in some well-defined circumstances (especially if the mother's life or health is seriously at risk) abortion — though bad — is still better than any other alternative.

## Questions for discussion

1. When do you think human life begins? How far does your answer to that question affect your views on abortion?
2. Can more be done to deal with the problems that cause requests for abortion?
3. Should terminally ill patients be allowed to end their lives if they want to?
4. What would be the dangers in legalizing euthanasia?

# Society's structures

## 16. Politics

In the last five chapters we have been looking at some of the
ways Christians are led by their faith to rescue society's *casualties*.
Now we move on a stage further, to explore the ways Christianity
relates to society's *structures*.

Brian Wren, a United Reformed church minister, explains the
difference by telling a modern parable:

> 'There was once a factory which employed thousands of
> people. Its production line was a miracle of modern engi-
> neering, turning out thousands of machines every day.
> The factory had a high accident rate. The complicated ma-
> chinery of the production line took little account of human
> error, forgetfulness or ignorance. Day after day, men came
> out of the factory with squashed fingers, cuts, bruises.
> Sometimes a man would lose an arm or a leg. Occasionally
> someone was electrocuted or crushed to death.
>
> Enlightened people began to see that something needed
> to be done. First on the scene were the churches. An
> enterprising minister organized a small first-aid tent out-
> side the factory gate. Soon, with the backing of the Council
> of Churches, it grew into a properly-built clinic, able to
> give first-aid to quite serious cases, and to treat minor
> injuries. The town council became interested, together
> with local bodies like the Chamber of Trade and the Rotary
> Club. The clinic grew into a small hospital, with modern
> equipment, an operating theatre, and a full-time staff of
> doctors and nurses. Several lives were saved. Finally, the
> factory management, seeing the good that was being done,
> and wishing to prove itself enlightened, gave the hospital

a small annual grant, and an ambulance to speed serious
cases from workshop to hospital ward.

But, year by year, as production increased, the accident
rate continued to rise. More and more people were hurt or
maimed. And, in spite of everything the hospital could do,
more and more people died from the injuries they had
received. Only then did some people begin to ask if it was
enough to treat people's injuries, while leaving untouched
the machinery that caused them.'

Christians have a clear duty to act as stretcher-bearers for
society's casualties. But does their faith also encourage them to
take a further step and work towards changing the social structures that cause the casualties in the first place? That is the
question Brian Wren is asking his readers to face.

**Political involvement**

By tackling 'the machinery', he means getting involved in politics.
When we think of politics, our minds go first to general elections,
manifestos and party political broadcasts. But political action covers a much larger area than that.

'Politics' has been defined as 'any activity concerned with the
decision-making, or government, of an organized group of people'. In this broad sense, even a local sports club has its politics.
A school certainly has. Whenever a parent-teacher association
meets to discuss the organization of a syllabus, or to draw up a
petition protesting against cuts in the education service, it is
'doing politics'. The introduction of examinations (whatever you
may think of them!) was itself a political move, designed by
teachers and others from various parts of the country as a protest
against the way university places and the best jobs were being
obtained by bribery or 'influence' of some other kind.

The Christian church in Britain and North America has often
been reluctant to involve itself in political action. This has earned
it criticism from inside as well as outside its membership. At the
beginning of the century, for example, Walter Rauschenbusch,
an American Baptist minister who earned himself the title 'Father
of the Social Gospel in America', complained: 'Ascetic Christianity called the world evil and left it. Humanity is waiting for a
revolutionary Christianity which will call the world evil and
change it.' Twenty years later, on this side of the Atlantic,

Professor Tawney felt the world was still waiting. Writing about industrial conflict, he commented that Christians 'relieved the wounded and comforted the dying, but they dared not enter the battle'.

The criticism is not completely fair. Historically, some of the most important social changes have resulted from political action spear-headed by Christians. The campaign to abolish slavery in Britain is perhaps the most obvious example. There have also been individual church leaders such as Archbishop William Temple and the American Dr Reinhold Niebuhr who have had enormous political influence during their lifetime. Today, as well, Christians in other parts of the world (such as South America and Eastern Europe) have played a prominent part in resisting political oppression.

Nevertheless, it is true that many Christians still fight shy of any kind of political involvement. Some use the 'world-denying' arguments we have already looked at in Chapter 11. Others accept that social care is a Christian responsibility, but remain unimpressed by Brian Wren's argument that social concern must find some sort of political expression. And there, of course, they have the support of many professional politicians who do not want the church 'interfering' in their business. As Enoch Powell once put it, the churches should restrict themselves to 'the sole reason and justification for their calling, the doctrine and sacraments of the Church'. After all, how would the bishops like it if the Trades Union Congress suggested changes in the creed?

## Jesus and politics

Was Jesus a politician? A few years ago, the American magazine *Time* devoted an issue to what it called 'The Jesus Revolution'. Among other things, it published these words of a 'Wanted' poster from a Christian underground newspaper:

---

WANTED


JESUS CHRIST
ALIAS: THE MESSIAH, THE SON OF
GOD, KING OF KINGS, LORD OF
LORDS, PRINCE OF PEACE, ETC.

---

* Notorious leader of an underground liberation movement
* Wanted for the following charges:
   –Practising medicine, winemaking and food distribution without a licence.
   –Associating with known criminals, radicals, subversives, prostitutes and street people.
   –Claiming to have the authority to make people into God's children.
   APPEARANCE: Typical hippie type — long hair, beard, robe, sandals.
* Hangs around slum areas, few rich friends, often sneaks out into the desert.
BEWARE: This man is extremely dangerous. His insidiously inflammatory message is particularly dangerous to young people who haven't been taught to ignore him yet. He changes men and claims to set them free.

WARNING: HE IS STILL AT LARGE!

Jesus was certainly born into a revolutionary atmosphere. The political climate of Judea in his day was as highly-charged as that of any South American republic today. Quite often he was forced to face the alternative of violent revolution. At least one, and possible five, of his inner ring of disciples were Zealots (the freedom-fighters of the time). Matthew tells how strongly he was tempted to become a political Messiah (see *Matthew* 4:8–9). And the crowds encouraged him to lead them in rebellion against the Roman occupying forces (see *John* 6:15).

It seems, however, that Jesus deliberately opted out of a revolutionary role. He rode into the capital city on an animal of peace (see *Mark* 11:1–10). A few days later he was arrested on a false charge, but he did not resist (see *Matthew* 26:47–56). He accepted the authority of his Roman judge (see *John* 19:10–11). And after his conviction and sentence, he went to his death without any token show of force or shout of defiance.

Jesus' example, especially the way that he faced his trial and death, strongly supports those who claim to be following his lead when they challenge social values without trying to smash or change social structures. His revolution, they maintain, was not political in nature but spiritual and moral.

Nevertheless, there is another side to the gospel story. The song Mary sang after she had become pregnant told of 'bringing down mighty kings from their thrones' and 'sending the rich away with empty hands' (*Luke* 1:51–53). In its own way the Magnificat (as this song is known) is far more revolutionary than the 'Red Flag'. Jesus himself struck the same revolutionary note at the beginning of his ministry when he applied the Old Testament prophet Isaiah's words to himself: 'He has sent me to proclaim liberty to the captives . . . to set free the oppressed' (*Luke* 4:18). And though there was no political demonstration at his death, the notice the Romans put on Jesus' cross showed that they, at least, regarded him as a political threat (see *Mark* 15:25–26).

In fairly recent times, a movement has grown up within the church called 'liberation theology'. Especially strong in South America, it aims to encourage political action on behalf of all oppressed people. In doing so, it claims to be following in Jesus' footsteps. He (it is argued) came into the world to revolutionize human life, so his followers should imitate him by revolutionizing the structures of society which shape human life. His aim was to redeem the world and to bring in God's Kingdom. Modern Christians, therefore, should have the same aim and work to establish God's rule in the world by all means available to them, including political ones.

It is possible, then, to come to very different conclusions by emphasizing separate aspects of Jesus' attitude to political involvement. If we put the whole picture of his life together, however, we find that he kept a very delicate balance between challenging those in authority (which he did) and rebelling against them (which he did not). His reply to a trick question about paying taxes showed how narrow a tight-rope he was walking. 'Pay the Emperor what belongs to the Emperor', he said, 'and pay God what belongs to God' (*Mark* 12:13–17).

**Protest and rebellion**

In his letter to the Romans, Paul takes up Jesus' word for 'pay' and uses it to set out the Christian citizen's political obligations in a little more detail (see *Romans* 13:7). The word itself is an unusual one. It really means 'pay back what you owe as a debt'. In Jesus' mind, as well as in Paul's, individuals are in debt to the state. They may not approve of the way the state uses its revenues (the Roman Christians' tax money possibly helped to buy instruments of torture used against them), but they must pay up all the same. They use the state amenities, and they must pay back what they owe.

Paul supports this obligation in a very striking way. 'You pay taxes', he writes, 'because the authorities are working for God when they fulfil their duties.' (*Romans* 13:6). In other words, the Christian sees God's authority behind the government's. 'Everyone must obey the state authorities, because no authority exists without God's permission, and the existing authorities have been put there by God' (verse 1). That belief makes the Christian think hard before supporting a revolution, because 'whoever opposes the existing authority opposes what God has ordered' (verse 2).

This confidence (that the *principle* of government is part of God's design for the world) comes through again and again in the Bible. In a political way, it expresses the belief that no government, however bad, is beyond God's control. As Jeremiah put it, speaking in God's name, 'It is I who by my great power and my outstretched arm have made the earth, with the men and the animals that are on the earth, and I give it to whomever it seems right to me. Now I have given all these lands into the hands of Nebuchadnezzar, the king of Babylon, my servant.' (*Jeremiah* 27:5). Nebuchadnezzar was as oppressive a ruler as the Roman Emperors whom the first Christians knew. He has his modern counterparts in the harsh communist and totalitarian regimes which make life hard for many Christians today.

God's *control*, however, is not the same as God's *approval*. The Bible certainly discourages impatient rebellion against state authorities. But it gives no encouragement to those who say, 'Christians must obey the government, because the government is always right.'

There are several examples of *civil disobedience* in both the Old Testament and the New. Daniel and his friends defied King Nebuchadnezzar (see *Daniel* 3:16–18); the apostles disobeyed the Jewish authorities (see *Acts* 4:18–20 and 5:27–29); and Paul staged the first Christian sit-in at the Philippi jail (see *Acts* 16:35–37). There are even more instances of *vocal protest* in the Bible. The prophet Nathan confronted King David after his adultery with Bathsheba (see 2 *Samuel* 12:1–15), while Elijah risked his life in exposing King Ahab (see 1 *Kings* 21:17–24), and John the Baptist lost his in criticizing King Herod's sex-life (see *Mark* 6:16–18).

On *violent revolution*, however, the Bible is silent. The first

Christians quickly gained for themselves the reputation of 'turning the world upside down' (*Acts* 17:6). But although civil disturbance often followed their preaching, they never provoked it deliberately. Even in the book of Revelation, with its grim picture of the state as a persecuting power, we find Christians preparing for martyrdom, not rebellion.

Liberation theologians explain this silence as a sign of the great culture-gap that separates biblical times from our own. The fact that the early Christians did not fight oppressive state powers by force is no reason, they say, why the church should not do so today. Thus church leaders in South America believe that they can best display the love of Christ by supporting revolutionary movements to overthrow political systems which prevent the hungry being fed and the naked clothed. It is not the freedom-fighters, they point out, who are bringing in the violence. They are simply responding to the aggressive force used by the authorities of the state.

Other Christians, probably the majority, believe that Christian involvement in politics should stop short of violence. Jacques Ellul, a French Professor of Law who played an active part in the Resistance Movement in World War 2, speaks for many when he writes: 'Christians who side with the oppressed and justify violence on their behalf cannot be counted among those who hunger and thirst for justice. . . . Once you start violence, you cannot get away from it. . . . It is impossible to distinguish between justified and unjustified violence, between violence that liberates and violence that enslaves.'

## Questions for discussion

1. What are the main political issues in your own neighbourhood at the moment?
2. Should the church stay out of politics?
3. How far is it right to go in opposing an unjust government?

# 17. Censorship and freedom

Censorship has always been unpopular, because no-one likes to feel restricted. Why should someone else tell me what I am allowed to see, hear or read? There may be a case for keeping some things away from very young children, but no teenager or adult wants a nanny!

Most of us have an obstinate streak to our nature, too. If something is censored, we want to know all about it. If the headmaster publicly bans a magazine from a school, it isn't long before there's a copy under every desk. When someone takes a film producer to court on an obscenity charge, everybody wants to see the film.

## What is censorship?

Censorship has three main targets. First, some pieces of information may be banned from general circulation *in the interests of state security*. This is why people who work in some jobs have to sign their agreement to keep the Official Secrets Act, and why the government sometimes slaps a 'D notice' on a news item to stop it being published by the press.

Secondly, some books, newspapers, plays, etc may be banned *to prevent violence*. If leaflets are distributed in the street which incite people to racial hatred, the police have power to confiscate them.

Thirdly, attempts are sometimes made to stop things reaching people's eyes and ears which are *immoral, offensive or blasphemous*. This is the type of censorship which causes most argument and disagreement.

Quite a number of old laws regulate printed material of this third kind. Most are hardly ever used today, but tonnes of pornographic photographs, magazines and books are still confiscated annually by customs officers at the docks under the Customs Consolidation Act 1876. Among more recent laws, two of the most important are the Post Office Act 1953, which makes it illegal to send obscene articles through the post, and the Obscene Publications Acts 1959 and 1964, which prohibit anything which 'tends to deprave or corrupt persons who are likely . . . to read, see or hear the matter contained or embodied in it'.

Because of the 'U', 'PG', '15' and '18' ratings you see on cinema posters, some people think that films are still censored. This, however, is not strictly true. The British Board of Film Censors (six men who work in a London office) has no legal power to stop or change any film it sees. Even so, a local council can ban cinemas in its district from showing certain films, whatever the ratings they have been given, if it wishes to do so.

The cases for and against censorship (especially of the third kind) are finely balanced. Here are the main arguments used by those on both sides of the debate.

**Arguments against censorship**

(i) *Obscenity is impossible to define.* Some people will find a particular object or article obscene, while others will find nothing wrong with it at all. We say 'beauty is in the eye of the beholder'. Perhaps the same is true of obscenity. It all depends how you look at things. As Paul wrote, in New Testament times, 'To the pure, all things are pure' (*Titus* 1:15).

If you banned everything which offended anyone, not much would be left. It is even doubtful whether the Bible or Shakespeare would survive. One critic (John Style) wrote about Shakespeare, for example: 'Barefaced obscenities, low vulgarities and nauseous vice so frequently figure and pollute his pages that we cannot but regret the luckless hour he became a writer for the stage.'

This is why (the argument goes) the Obscene Publications Act is so unsatisfactory. Everything hangs on the personal opinions of 12 men and women sitting on a jury. The authors of books or films are put in an impossible position, when they cannot know for certain in advance whether or not they are producing something illegal.

(ii) *Pornography helps people.* Not so long ago, two important bodies, the Arts Council in Great Britain and a Presidential Commission in the United States, investigated the effects of pornography on those who read and saw it. Both came up with the conclusion that no harmful effects could be proved at all.

Before and since then, some psychiatrists have argued that a number of their patients have actually been helped by pornography. Some lonely people, they reported, had found sexual release that way. Others had found satisfaction in reading pornographic magazines and doing things in their imagination which would have been highly dangerous and harmful if they had tried to do them in real life.

(iii) *Censorship threatens personal freedom.*   People should be free, it is argued, to see, hear and read what they want to in private. The law should only interfere if there is a direct threat to the safety of society — and that does not often happen. Minority groups must not be allowed to impose their opinions on the majority, nor should a minority group be robbed of its freedom to live and behave in the way it prefers, if no one else is put at risk.

One famous film producer protested, when he was accused of screening obscenity, 'An audience has the right to choose to see perversion if it wants to.' After all, cinema-goers can go somewhere else — just as viewers can turn off their T.V., and shoppers need not buy a pornographic magazine.

(iv) *Censorship does not produce its intended results.*   The whole object of censoring something is to stop people seeing, hearing or reading it. But, human nature being what it is, the very worst thing you can do if you want to stop something is to ban it. If a film producer is taken to court, he or she can be sure that whatever the outcome of the case, somewhere, somehow, his or her film will be a box-office success.

Many would argue that the American attempt before World War 2 to ban alcohol failed for exactly this reason. All that happened was that drink became more expensive, and the profits funded crime syndicates which still thrive today.

**Arguments for censorship**

Those who think some kind of censorship is necessary support their case in three main ways:

(i) *Pornography exploits and degrades.*   This is especially so in the case of women. A recent Gallup Poll asked the question, 'Do you think pornography degrades women?' Sixty per cent of those who replied said that it did.

Pornography degrades women, it is argued, because it reduces them from people to sex-objects. The nude in the girlie magazine is not a person. She is there as a hunk of flesh for use by men as a thrill-machine.

Some would add that pornography also devalues sex and love. Instead of being something intimately private, sex is exploited commercially. And love is robbed of its richness by being put on the same level as lust.

(ii) *Pornography is harmful.* Everything that we see and hear has some effect on us. If that were not so, firms would not spend millions of pounds each year on advertising. And evidence is fast accumulating that the harmful effects of pornography far outweigh the benefits it is meant to bring to a few.

For one thing, pornography makes people less sensitive. Some things, such as rape and violent crime, should shock us. But after watching several scenes of violence on television each week, our minds get numb. Sexual assault and mugging do not sicken us quite as much as they used to.

Some people actually imitate what they see on film or read in print. Recent research has shown that the number of serious sex offences rises in countries which have abolished censorship on pornography. Some recent trials for rape in Britain illustrate this. At the end of one, the judge commented: 'It is often said that pornography really does not cause any evil results. On the evidence of this case, but for the literature this matter would never have arisen.'

(iii) *Censorship protects freedom.* As we have seen, those who want to abolish censorship argue that it threatens personal freedom. But that, say their opponents, is simply not true.

As evidence, they ask us to compare other areas of life where our freedom is protected by laws which stop people doing certain things. Those who live in the inner city are only allowed to burn smokeless fuel, so everyone can breathe the air more freely. Our freedom of speech is protected, not threatened, by laws which prohibit slander and libel. And the freedom of ethnic minority groups is safeguarded by the Race Relations Act, which 'censors' racist behaviour.

All these laws defend our freedom by restraining social menaces who would rob us of it if they could. They all involve
censorship of one kind or another.

So why, the argument goes, do we object to laws which are
designed to protect the community from *moral* harm?

## Bible teaching

What, then, is the 'Christian' view of censorship? The Bible does
not tell us in so many words, but it does offer us some useful
guidelines. Here are one or two of the more important ones.

(i) *The meaning of freedom.*   Jesus stressed the importance of freedom. He taught that only Christians can know what 'being free'
really means. 'If the Son makes you free', he said (meaning
himself), 'you will be really free' (*John* 8:36).

But Jesus did not teach that freedom means 'being free to do
what you like'. When we talk about freedom, we often mean
being free *from* restraints of various kinds. When Jesus talked
about it, he meant being free *to* do something worthwhile and
constructive. That is why Paul defined freedom like this: 'As for
you, my brothers, you were called to be free. But do not let this
freedom become an excuse for letting your physical desires control you. Instead, let love make you serve one another' (*Galatians*
5:13).

If you think of freedom as 'free *from*', you will be biased
against all censorship. But if you think of it more as 'free *to*', you
may welcome the kind of restraint that helps you to serve others
better.

(ii) *The value of control.*   In his second New Testament letter,
Peter writes like this about the porn-merchants he knew: 'They
promise people freedom, while they themselves are slaves of
depravity — for a man is slave to whatever has mastered him'
(*2 Peter* 2:19). Writing to Corinth, a city notorious in those times
for sexual vice, Paul adds, 'I will not be mastered by anything'
(*1 Corinthians* 6:12).

In most people, the sex-drive is one of the strongest instincts
they know. It is also one of the ugliest sides of human nature if
it gets out of control and is not harnessed in the service of love.
If censorship is so severe that it creates the impression that all
sex is dirty, something has gone wrong. But if pornography

*Freedom of speech is a precious human right. These striking shipyard workers in Gdansk, Poland, were soon silenced by martial law. What are the dangers of suppressing free speech? What consequences might there be, both to individuals and the state?*

threatens to make us slaves to sex, some control of it is essential
— in the interests of our freedom.

(iii) *The importance of the thought-life.*   In Jesus' day, most teachers
said, 'If you want to live a good life, you must stop doing bad
things and start doing good ones.' Jesus dug far deeper into
human nature than that. The roots of bad conduct, he taught,
are in the mind and heart: 'For from the inside, from a person's
heart, come the evil ideas which lead him to do immoral things.'
(*Mark* 7:21). So, according to Jesus, it is not much good for a man
to congratulate himself because he has never committed adultery
in the flesh, if he does it every day in his imagination (see *Matthew*
5:27–28).

The Bible is positive about the thought-life, too. 'Let God
transform you inwardly by a complete change of your mind',
wrote Paul (*Romans* 12:2). 'Fill your minds with those things that
are good and that deserve praise: things that are true, noble,
right, pure, lovely, and honourable.' (*Philippians* 4:8). The message is plain enough, even if the language sounds rather quaint!

Pornography feeds the mind with something. If we agree that
the 'something' is bad, Christianity will not allow us to shrug it
off by saying 'My mind is my own business — so long as I don't
act out my thoughts, no one can complain.' Censorship alone,
on the other hand, does not feed the mind with anything at all.
Biblical teaching makes Christians look for better, alternative
mind-fillers, that the censor cannot provide.

(iv) *The need to protect the weak.*   Some people are more vulnerable to some temptations than others. The Bible insists that the
strong should always make allowances for the weak (see, for
example, *Matthew* 18:6 and *1 Corinthians* 8:9).

Pornography has little effect on some people (apart, perhaps,
from making them laugh). But for others it packs a terrible punch.
'Addiction to pornography is like a cancer of the mind', one
doctor writes. We cannot, of course, ban everything that is a
source of temptation to someone. If we did, there would be very
little left to see or read. But the Bible encourages Christians to
think twice about allowing something to continue unchecked just
because it does not trouble *them*.

## Questions for discussion

1. Is censorship always a bad thing?
2. How much influence do newspapers and films have on people?
3. Who should society's censors be? How should their powers be limited?

# 18. Relationships at work

In many countries, it is known as the 'British disease' — the bad relations between working people which can eventually throttle the life out of a nation's economy. Apart from a tiny fringe of militants who have political reasons for stirring up trouble, no-one really wants civil war in industry. Yet, week after week, the television news brings us fresh evidence of industrial unrest.

It is all very puzzling. At the end of six months' 'industrial education' Prince Charles confessed, 'The more factories I go to, the more questions I ask, the more union representatives I meet, the more shop committees I attend, the more board meetings I sit on, the more managers I listen to — the more confused I become!'

Most of the problems which arise from bad relations at work have a very modern ring about them. This makes it difficult to apply traditional Christian teaching in a relevant way. The Bible, for example, has no help to offer on such things as lack of investment, new technology or low productivity! Words such as 'strike', 'go-slow' and 'work to rule' just do not feature in either the Old Testament or the New. The conditions of working life were so different then. Large groups of people did not work in vast multi-national concerns without any personal contact with their bosses. Nor did directors share their interests over dozens of different companies.

Nevertheless, the Bible does have some very basic things to say about working relationships and, while the outward shape of the problems may have changed, the central core (what Prince Charles called 'the one overriding factor in industrial life — the human being') is still very much the same.

By far the most prominent feature of biblical teaching in this area of social life is its call for *honesty* and *justice*. And Christian commentators find no difficulty in applying these two demands to the world of business and industry today.

### Commercial relations

In Jesus' day, the temple at Jerusalem was notorious for the way it exploited its monopoly on money-changing and the sale of sacrificial victims. Every worshipper had to pay a temple tax in special currency, and the rate of exchange was fixed in such a way that most customers lost half a day's wage on the deal. Doves for sacrifice were available in the temple precincts, too — but only at a vastly inflated price. A dove could be bought outside for a fraction of the cost, but the temple inspectors had a nasty habit of rejecting birds that had not been purchased at the temple stalls.

This swindling of pilgrims provoked Jesus to the most violent action of his life. 'He overturned the tables of the money-changers and the stools of those who sold pigeons', Mark reports, as he accused the temple tradesmen of turning the house of prayer into 'a hideout for thieves' (*Mark* 11:15–17).

The Old Testament also aims some strong words at shady business practice. 'All who cheat with unjust weights and measurements are detestable to the Lord your God', warns the law of *Deuteronomy* (25:16). 'Shall I say "Good!" to all your merchants with their bag of deceitful weights?', echoes the prophet Micah. 'How could God be just while saying that?' (*Micah* 6:11).

The conditions of commercial life have changed, but it is not hard to apply these biblical principles across the gap of the centuries. Methods of cheating customers may have become more sophisticated over the years, but they are really only variations on the same theme.

Multi-nationals may exploit their monopolies. Some High Street stores may mislead customers with 'Sale' notices, unrealistic delivery dates and guarantees that are not quite what they seem when you read the small print. The fact that the vast majority of these businesses are thoroughly respectable, in the sense that they operate within the letter of the law, cannot conceal the fact that their operations sometimes blur the edges of honesty. There were few more respectable places to conduct your business in Jesus' day than the temple in Jerusalem.

If the Old Testament prophets had lived in the twentieth century, the advertising industry might have been one of their main targets. This is not to suggest that many advertisers are deliberately dishonest. Occasionally the truth is stretched to breaking point, but in Britain watch-dogs such as the Advertising

Standards Association and the Independent Broadcasting Authority keep a sharp eye on commercials which are not (in the words of the I.B.A. Code of Standards and Practice) 'legal, decent, honest and truthful'.

Some advertisements, however, do mislead customers in more subtle ways. Often, for example, advertisers promise side-benefits which they cannot possibly deliver. Sometimes these are so obviously ridiculous that no-one can possibly be deceived (like the very funny claims made for the beer 'which reaches parts other beers cannot reach'). But occasionally they pack a very powerful emotional punch.

An appeal to status symbols comes high in this category. It is all very well to say that no-one in his or her right mind would buy a new car in the belief that *all* the neighbours will turn green with envy when they see it, or use a new shampoo because it will make *every* member of the opposite sex turn his head. But the suggestion can be enough to sell the product, as both the manufacturer and the advertiser know.

Even more serious, from the Christian point of view, is the set of values these advertisements reflect. They appeal, very frequently, to qualities such as envy, greed, vanity and pride which the Christian gospel black-lists. No one, of course, suggests that the advertisers actually create these attitudes in people's minds, but by playing on them skilfully they are bound to reinforce their grip. Try reconciling Jesus' words, 'Watch out and guard yourselves from every kind of greed; because a person's true life is not made up of the things he owns' (*Luke* 12:15), with the message behind this evening's television commercials.

**Industrial relations**

As far as we know, Jesus had very little to say about relations between employers and employees. He made many powerful enemies, however, by standing up for society's underdogs. According to Luke, his first sermon in his home-town of Nazareth was based on Isaiah's prophecy that the Messiah would 'set free the oppressed' (*Luke* 4:16–19).

Isaiah and the other Old Testament prophets spoke out time and time again, often at great risk to their lives, in support of the oppressed. Victimized workers were prominent among the oppressed people they knew. Because the scales were weighted so heavily in favour of the employer in Bible times, the prophets

often sound like modern trade union spokesmen when they de-
nounce the exploitation of working people by unscrupulous
bosses. Malachi, for example, brackets 'those who cheat employees out of their wages' with 'those who take advantage of
widows, orphans and foreigners' (*Malachi* 3:5). Jeremiah, too,
calls down God's judgement on 'the man who builds his house
by injustice and enlarges it by dishonesty; who makes his
countrymen work for nothing and does not pay their wages'
(*Jeremiah* 22:13).

The principle of the just wage comes out strongly in the New
Testament as well as the Old. Jesus himself said 'the worker
deserves his wages' (*Luke* 10:7), and James sounds very much
like an Old Testament prophet when he exposes wealthy farmers
who do not pay their labour force fairly. 'Listen to their complaints!', he thunders. 'The cries of those who gather in your
crops have reached the ears of God, the Lord Almighty' (*James*
5:4).

The Old Testament law adds an interesting tail-piece to this
demand for justice in wage-payments: 'Do not hold back the
wages of someone you have hired, not even for one night. . . .
Each day before sunset pay him for that day's work; he needs
the money and has counted on getting it' (*Leviticus* 19:13; *Deuteronomy* 24:15). In other words, when you are paying a poor man
for his services, delay is fraud — an interesting principle to apply
when large firms pay their small producers two months or more
in arrears to suit their own profit and convenience.

In the face of this very strong insistence on prompt and fair
payment of wages in the Bible, it is strange to find church leaders
opposing the modern trade union movement in its never-ending
fight to win better pay and conditions for its members. Lord
Fisher of Lambeth, for example, wrote in a national newspaper,
in the year of his retirement as Archbishop of Canterbury, 'I
think it is an unrighteous thing ever to strike for money, except
possibly when you are starving.'

A strike is, after all, just an organized withdrawal of labour.
As Joseph Hume said, in a House of Commons speech at the
turn of the century, 'Labour is the commodity of men, as capital
is of the masters, and both are allowed to obtain the best terms
they can.' It is no more unfair for employ*ees* to withdraw their
labour when it is under-priced, than it is for employ*ers* to keep
their goods from the markets and shops when they are not getting a just return for them.

That is not, of course, to whitewash *all* strike action. Some strikes are selfish, in that they ignore the third parties who suffer as a result. When trade union leaders go on television and express their regret for any inconvenience their industrial action might cause to the general public, it is sometimes hard to believe them — especially if it is the power workers who go on strike during the winter, the air traffic controllers during the summer holiday season, or the teachers just before exam time. The principle of neighbour-love that Jesus taught, especially in the parable of the Good Samaritan, makes it wrong for one group of people to advance their own interests by making others suffer.

Again, a cry for justice may simply be a smoke-screen for greed. When some soldiers asked John the Baptist 'What about us? What are we to do?', his answer was, 'Don't take money from anyone by force or accuse anyone falsely. Be content with your pay.' (*Luke* 3:14). Soldiers in those days were powerful people. They could use bullying tactics to increase their take-home pay whenever they wanted. Their counterparts today, perhaps, are the more powerful unions who can hold the country to ransom by the threat of going on strike.

Any kind of hostile industrial action, however, is like a pain which indicates the presence of a disease. And most industrialists agree that the disease which poisons working relations most seriously today is failure to respect the value of the individual.

We find symptoms of this disease on both sides of modern industry. On the management side, workers are sometimes treated as little more than clock numbers, human tools to be used in the business of increasing profit. On the labour side, the conscience of the individual trade union member is often stifled by 'closed shop' policies and by aggressive picketing techniques.

Here, probably, Christian teaching makes its most important contribution. The value of the individual is a basic principle of Christian belief. Jesus underlined it when he described himself as a shepherd who is not content with 99 sheep when he ought to have a hundred. He leaves the main group to rescue the one.

In practical terms, this means that the individual's conscience must always be respected (even if the strength of the group's position is weakened). It means, too, that the individual's well-being must always be set above his or her function as a unit in profit-making. A Code of Conduct drawn up by a group of Christian businessmen expresses the principle very clearly: 'I believe that each individual is significant to God. I will therefore treat each person fully and considerately as one needing a satisfactory occupation, seeking his maximum personal development and just remuneration.'

The Christian approach to working relations, then, majors on the twin values of *honesty* and *justice*. Inevitably, Christian voices are most often heard in denouncing *dis*honest and *un*just policies and practices. There is, however, a positive side to the protests. At the heart of the Christian gospel is the message of reconciliation. Above everything else, therefore, Christians are called to be reconcilers, mending broken relationships and encouraging co-operation between those who are more inclined to fight.

## Questions for discussion

1. How much could industrial relations be improved if Christian ideals were applied?
2. How far do advertisements reinforce bad qualities in our characters?
3. Do you think picketing (during a strike) is immoral? (Pickets are supposed to persuade people, using peaceful means, not to work or deliver goods during the strike.)

# 19. Ecology and conservation

If someone got into your home while you were at school today and smashed everything up, you wouldn't shrug your shoulders and do nothing. You would do your best to see that the vandal was caught, and then take extra precautions to make sure it did not happen again. But suppose one day you did the same thing yourself — not in somebody else's home, but in your own? If you started chopping your bed up and heaving chairs through the kitchen window, the rest of the family would probably sit on you until the doctor arrived!

A crazy idea? Not altogether, say the ecologists, because this is exactly what humankind has been doing for years. Our home is the world, but instead of taking care of it, we have been smashing it up. Soon it will not be fit to live in, and then what will we do?

**The problem**

Wherever we look, we see signs of the same problem. Take a trip through West Africa, for example, and you will pass through mile upon mile of desert. A great deal of this dry, barren land grew vegetation not so long ago, but people allowed their animals to overgraze it. The result is that in this and other parts of the world the desert's edges are creeping outwards (at the rate of about twenty miles a year, the naturalists tell us). So people are destroying their own food cupboard.

In many ways, too, modern industrial society is adding to the ecological problem. Precious natural resources are being swallowed up, far too rapidly for replacement. Some, like oil, cannot be replaced at all. Our use of trees provides a good example of what is happening. Whole forests are being cut down to satisfy the printing trade's increasing demand for paper, with the result that birds and animals lose their habitats. Ultimately, climatic changes take place and the land surface itself is eroded.

Disposing of waste is another major aspect of the problem. Modern fertilizers increase our food crops, and detergents make cleaning easier, but when the rain washes their remnants into the rivers, changes take place in the water vegetation. These in turn choke the flow of water, lower its oxygen content and turn our waterways into stinking sewers.

Other chemical waste causes even greater problems. Some poisons used in insecticides have been found in fish brought ashore to be sold in the world's markets. Once again, it seems as though people *are* determined to break up their own home. And we still have to work out a fail-safe method to dispose of waste from nuclear power stations.

Technology is certainly fighting back. In the Middle East, desert is being reclaimed by new agricultural methods. London, too, has lost its famous smoke-fogs since the Clean Air Acts came into force, and you can now wander along the banks of the Thames without a peg on your nose. It comes as quite a shock to be reminded that 150 years ago special curtains, impregnated with calcium chloride, were put up at the windows of the Houses of Parliament to mask the awful smell from London's famous river!

Nevertheless, on a world scale, the problem of the environment is still getting bigger. A few years ago the Secretary-General of the United Nations described 'the crisis of the human environment' as 'a crisis of world-wide proportions'. 'It is becoming apparent', he said, 'that, if current trends continue, the future of life on earth could be endangered.' Against that background, then, let us explore what the Bible has to say about humans and nature.

## Humans and nature in the Bible

The Bible teaches very clearly that human destiny is tied up closely with the environment. The two sides of the creation story in Genesis make that plain. When God created Adam, he gave him special responsibility for his surroundings (see *Genesis* 2:15). And when he rebelled against God, the results affected the environment as well as the human race. 'Because of what *you* have done', the Lord said, '*the ground* will be under a curse.' (*Genesis* 3:17)

The rest of the Old Testament tells how God loved humanity back to himself. Again, at each of the key points in the story, people and their environment are closely bound up together. After the Flood (when nature suffered as well as humanity), God made his covenant not just with humans but with 'every living creature that is with you' (*Genesis* 9:12). And out in the Sinai desert, when Moses received the Ten Commandments, the sabbath law laid it down that the livestock should enjoy a day off each week along with the human members of the household (see *Exodus* 20:10).

Most significantly of all, when Moses' people reached the promised land, God gave them laws for the care of the environment alongside laws governing their social life. Conservation was the key-note. Fruit trees were to be preserved, even when wood was badly needed for the war effort (see *Deuteronomy* 20:19–20). Every seventh year, the land itself must be given a rest from intensive cultivation, even though its owners longed to harvest the corn that had seeded itself and the grapes from the unpruned vines (see *Leviticus* 25:1–7, 18–22).

Over in the New Testament, Jesus illustrated this call to conservation in much of his teaching. He identified the good shepherd as the man who values his animals so highly that he would risk his life to save theirs (unlike the person who is only in the job for the money — see *John* 10:11–12). And he taught about God's care for the individual by telling the story of the farmer who hunted everywhere for one lost animal, even though he had 99 others safe and well on the hillside (see *Matthew* 18:12–14).

Paul adds the finishing touch in a prediction of nature's fate at the end of the world. 'All creation', he writes, 'is waiting patiently and hopefully for that future day when God will glorify His children. For on that day thorns and thistles, sin, death and decay that overcame the world against its will . . . will all disappear, and the world around us will share in the glorious freedom from sin which God's children enjoy.' (*Romans* 8:19–21).

According to the Bible, humans and their environment are bound up closely in their joint destiny from the world's beginning to its end. In the light of this teaching, Christians cannot have a 'humans only' view of the world. Those who just shrug their shoulders when they see animals suffering, forests carved up and land spoiled do not share their Creator's outlook on the rest of creation.

## Humans as managers

When humans face nature, they face something like themselves, because they are part of it.

Back in the fourth century, Bishop Chrysostom of Constantinople spelt it out like this: 'Surely we ought to show them (animals) great kindness and gentleness for many reasons, but, above all, *because they are of the same origin as ourselves.*' According to the creation story, it was Adam and Eve's proud desire to rise above their creatureliness and 'become as gods' that drew from God the stern reminder 'You are dust, and to dust you shall return.' (*Genesis* 3:19).

In this sense, a person is on the same level as a dog or a tree. But that is only half of the biblical story. The first chapters of Genesis also explain that God made humans *managers* of the rest of creation (see *Genesis* 1:27–29, 3:23 and 9:1–2). The author of Psalm 8 catches the themes of humanity's tininess (as creatures) and their greatness (as managers of the world) superbly, when he writes:

'When I look at the sky, which you have made,
at the moon and the stars, which you set in their places —
what is man, that you think of him;
mere man, that you care for him?

Yet you made him inferior only to yourself;
you crowned him with glory and honour.
You appointed him ruler over everything you made;
you placed him over all creation' (*Psalms* 8:3–6).

As creation's managers, people have two main responsibilities, according to the Bible. First, they must *conserve* the world's resources. Because they are managers of the world, not owners, its resources are not theirs to squander. The Bible makes it clear that God is still in charge of everything (see, for example, *Psalms* 24:1), and that people are accountable to him for any abuse or waste. That is why Christians are often to be found leading conservation projects to limit pollution, recycle basic materials such as paper and glass, and distribute foodstocks more fairly. It is all part of the manager's job.

Secondly, people must *use* the world's resources to their best possible effect. Good management does not stop with conservation. In Jesus' parable of the talents, the servant who conserved his master's money, but made no use of it, was blamed for his efforts, not congratulated (see *Matthew* 25:14–30). That is why Christians are also to be found at the head of scientific research and technological development. Those who want to put the clock back and live the 'simple life' without silicon chips are not living more closely to God, according to biblical teaching. They are simply being bad managers of the resources he has given them to use.

## Good and bad management

Armed with this biblical teaching, Christians see many of the world's environmental problems as the results of bad management.

Some are due to people's selfish failure to *conserve* the world's resources. What does it matter, people ask, if forests are destroyed in South America, so long as we get our Sunday papers? Who cares that oil supplies are limited, provided there is enough left to run *our* cars in *our* life-time? A few years ago, forty million fish died in the River Rhine, all because each country through which the river passes discharged poisonous waste into its waters at their downstream borders. As the American Christian writer Francis Schaeffer commented, 'These are the two factors that lead to the destruction of our environment: money and time — or, to say it another way, greed and hate.'

Seeing how harshly people can abuse their environment, some have turned to Eastern religions for help. Most of these put humanity and nature on the same level. We share a common 'life force', they claim, with the rest of the animal world. Therefore we must never take the life of an animal, either to feed or clothe ourselves or to protect our health.

The great Christian missionary, Albert Schweitzer, came very close to this point of view when he refused to kill flies in his operating theatre. But this, too, is really bad management, because it fails to *make full use* of the world's resources. Jesus set a very high value on the life of animals, but he never put them on the same level as people. 'A man is worth much more than a sheep!', he told his disciples (*Matthew* 12:12; see also *Luke* 12:6–7).

How, then, can we strike the right balance between *conserving* the world's resources and *using* them rightly? It is far from easy,

*These cliffs have been made by cows. In some parts of the world rich pasture has become desert through over-grazing. Soil becomes eroded. Forests die. Have we a duty to stop this damage to the environment? What are the problems?*

but here, to end the chapter, are one or two ways this biblical teaching might be applied today. If nothing else, these suggestions will start you debating!

(i) *Pest control.*   It is right to kill ants in the kitchen, to safeguard human health, but wrong to stamp on them in a walk through the woods, where they are not a health hazard.

(ii) *Trees.*   It is right to cut a tree down if its wood is needed to build a house, but wrong if it is simply in the way of a new road which could be re-routed.

(iii) *Killing animals.*   It is right to kill animals for food, or to protect other livestock, but not in the name of sport or to provide luxury goods such as furs.

(iv) *Vivisection.*   It is right to use animals for medical research if there are no other ways of testing new drugs or surgical techniques, but wrong if alternative methods are available, even if those are more expensive.

(v) *Farming.*   Rearing animals for market is right, so long as it is done in ways that cause them no discomfort and respect their dignity. Methods such as force-feeding geese to provide pâté, on the other hand, or rearing calves in semi-darkness to provide white veal, are wrong, and these products should be boycotted.

(vi) *Fuel.*   Using a car which is no larger than needed and economical on fuel is right, but choosing one because of its 'performance' or status value is a waste of resources, and therefore wrong.

What do *you* think?

**Questions for discussion**

1. How aware are we of the dangers caused by people's abuse of their surroundings?
2. How far would the ecologists' problems be solved if the Christian ideals of good management were followed?
3. Have the problems which threaten the world come about

through humans' ignorance, because of their selfishness — or for some other reason?

4. How far do you agree with the six examples of 'balance' at the end of the chapter?

# World affairs

## 20. World poverty

An African student described world poverty to me in a vivid way. 'It is like an iceberg floating in a hot sea', he said. 'It ought to melt away and disappear, but it doesn't.'

The world still has enough resources to meet the needs of everyone who lives in it, and yet a large number of its inhabitants are living on or below the poverty-line. There is enough food for everybody, but many people go to bed each night hungry. Like an iceberg in a hot sea, the problem ought not to exist — but it does.

**The facts of poverty**

In 1980, a group of international statesmen and economic experts led by Willy Brandt, former Chancellor of West Germany, published a report on world poverty called *North-South. A Programme for Survival*. As the title of their report suggests, they divided the world into two camps. The 'North' belongs to the developed, industrial nations of North America, Western Europe, the U.S.S.R., and (despite geography!) Australia and New Zealand. The 'South' consists of the under-developed or developing countries of Africa, Central and South America, South-East Asia and Arabia.

Here are some of the facts these world leaders collected:
(i) The North has only one-quarter of the world's population, but receives four-fifths of the world's income.
(ii) The North's standard of living is forty times higher than the South's, and the gap is still widening.
(iii) The North owns 90 per cent of the world's manufacturing industry.

(iv) People in the U.S.A. use as much fertilizer on their gardens and golf courses as the people of India do for everything, including their farmland.

(v) In the North, the average person spends only 20 per cent of his or her income on food. In the South, the figure is 80 per cent.

(vi) The infant mortality rate is 10 times higher in the South than it is in the North. In just one year (1978), 12 million children under the age of five died of starvation or malnutrition in poorer countries.

In these and other ways the world is divided between the rich nations and the poor. But the Brandt Commission also discovered the same split between wealth and poverty *within the nations of the South themselves*. In a typical developing country, they found that some people enjoyed a very high standard of living (especially government officials and agents of multi-national companies), while others starved. In Mexico, for example, just 20 per cent of the population receive 64 per cent of the nation's income. The distribution of land often shows up this kind of inequality most sharply. It is not unusual, the Commission discovered, for less than 10 per cent of a poor country's population to own more than half of the productive land.

If we ask why poverty cripples so many nations of the South, we can find answers of several different kinds. *The arms race* certainly absorbs a lot of money which might be diverted to help the poor. In an average year, the South spends 14 million dollars on weapons bought from the North. The price of one tank would save four thousand tonnes of rice annually, through improved storage facilities. It would be possible to set up 40 thousand village pharmacies for the cost of a single jet fighter. Nevertheless, poor countries prefer to buy tanks and planes than food and medicine.

*Population growth* has not helped either. The experts have calculated that about one million babies are born into the world every five days, most of them in the South. It is an ironical fact that those countries with the least food have the highest birthrates.

*International trade conditions* also drive the wedge between the rich and the poor deeper and deeper. Most poor nations depend on exporting raw materials for their economic survival. Zambia, for instance, relies on copper for 95 per cent of its export earnings, while Mauritius and Gambia have little to sell apart from their sugar and groundnuts. Countries such as these are completely at the mercy of importers from the North for the prices they get for their exports. And if they try to sell manufactured goods themselves, they are usually priced out of world markets by the tariffs and taxes that the wealthier nations impose to protect their own producers.

The *level of aid* the North provides for the South has fallen, making the plight of the poor even worse. Several years ago, the better-off countries agreed at the United Nations to contribute 0.7 per cent of their gross national product (G.N.P.) annually as development aid, but the average contribution today is less than half that figure. There are often strings attached to aid programmes, too, which benefit the donors more than the recipients.

Finally, there are *cultural* factors which play a part in keeping the gap between rich and poor wide open. In some nations of the South, education is not available to women. This obviously robs such countries of valuable human resources. It is also a sad fact that in some parts of the world hard work is not considered a virtue, though one must add that people cannot work hard on empty stomachs! Poverty is a vicious circle.

**The Bible and the poor**

There is nothing new, of course, in the experience of poverty. No-one contradicted Jesus when he said, 'You will always have poor people with you' (*Mark* 14:7). And though the social conditions of biblical times were very different from ours, the way the Bible tells its readers to treat the poor still provides Christians with guidelines today.

God supports the poor. That is the starting-point of the Old Testament's teaching on this theme. 'Lord', sings the Psalmist, 'I know that you defend the cause of the poor and the rights of the needy.' (*Psalms* 140:12). 'When you give to the poor', adds the book of Proverbs, it is like lending to the Lord, and the Lord will pay you back.' (*Proverbs* 19:17).

It is God's own nature and his example that lie behind the numerous laws of the Old Testament which favour the poor. Among them, the rules about tithing and gleaning were especially important. Every third year, the Israelite family had to give a tenth of its produce or earnings (that is, a tithe) to the poor (see *Deuteronomy* 14:27–29). And when the farmer harvested his fields, he had to leave the corn at the edge (the gleanings) for the needy to collect free of charge (see *Leviticus* 19:9–10).

The Old Testament law even had its own method for beating the 'poverty trap'. In Israelite society, as in many others today, there was a tendency for the rich to get richer and the poor poorer. To stop this trend, the law laid it down that every fiftieth year should be celebrated as a 'jubilee'. In it, all outstanding debts were to be cancelled, all slaves released, and every piece of property that had been sold was to be restored to its original owner (see *Leviticus* 25:8–17).

When Jesus came, one of the ways he described his aim as the Messiah was 'to bring good news to the poor' and 'to set free the oppressed' (*Luke* 4:18). He actually quoted those words from one of the Old Testament prophets. These prophets had been very outspoken in condemning those who oppressed the poor (see, for instance, *Amos* 2:6–7 and *Isaiah* 1:16–17).

But Jesus went even further than these prophets had done. For one thing, he taught that God would punish *neglect* of the poor. In his parable of the rich man and the beggar, the rich man ended up in hell for failing to help the down-and-out on his doorstep. He had never harmed him. He had simply ignored him (see *Luke* 16:19–31). Similarly, in the scene Jesus painted of God's final judgement, those who stand condemned include people who had failed to meet the needs of the hungry, the poor, the lonely, the cold and the sick (see *Matthew* 25:31–46).

Then, secondly, Jesus taught that genuine *love* will compel Christians to help the poor. That comes out very clearly in the parable of the Good Samaritan (*Luke* 10:25–37). Later, John captured the spirit of Jesus' teaching in this parable exactly when he wrote, 'If a rich person sees his brother in need, yet closes his heart against his brother, how can he claim that he loves God? My children, our love should not be just words and talk; it must be true love, which shows itself in action.' (*1 John* 3:17–18).

Spurred on by the teaching and example of Jesus, the first Christians earned themselves a big reputation for generosity, 'They all shared with one another everything they had', reports Luke. And the result was, 'there was no-one in the group who was in need.' (*Acts* 4:32, 34). It was not long before the Emperor complained peevishly in Rome, 'The godless Galileans nourish our poor in addition to their own; while ours get no care from us.'

### Tackling world poverty today

Armed with these biblical guidelines, Christians cannot sit back
and watch the world's poverty trap close on its victims. To meet
Christ's demands for love and justice, action is needed at three
levels.

1. *Personal lifestyle.*   Because God supports the poor and identi-
fies himself with them, Christians will want to do the same. With
Jesus' warning about neglecting the poor ringing in his or her
ears, no Christian dare live as if world poverty did not exist.

   The obvious way individual Christians in the rich North can
show care for the poor is by accepting a lower standard of living
themselves. If enough Christians did this, giving away the money
they did not actually need for life's necessities, quite large funds
would be available for development aid in other countries. One
American Professor has calculated that if everyone in the North
ate 10 per cent less meat, enough grain (now used for animal
fodder) would be released to feed 60 million people in the South.

   There is great power in a good example. The Bible finds the
root of the poverty problem in ordinary people's attitudes. Greed
and selfishness are the main culprits, according to Jesus. If Christians were to challenge these attitudes today by being more generous and by living more simply, the example they set could
have a strong moral influence in world society.

2. *Political and economic reform.*   Many people, however, would
say that setting a good personal example is not enough. The gap
between the North and the South is being maintained and
widened, they point out, by the structures of world trade. The
problem, therefore, must be tackled at the international level.

   From a Christian point of view, support for this approach can
be found in God's command to humans to be managers of the
world's resources. We were thinking of this in an earlier chapter.
The Bible teaches that the resources of the world belong to God
(see *Psalms* 24:1), and that he has given humans the responsibility
to use them rightly (see *Genesis* 1:28). According to Jesus, the
managers' main duty is to make sure that the resources under
their control are distributed fairly (see *Luke* 12:42). Today, it is the
politicians, the economists and the managing directors of multi-
national firms who have most power to develop and distribute

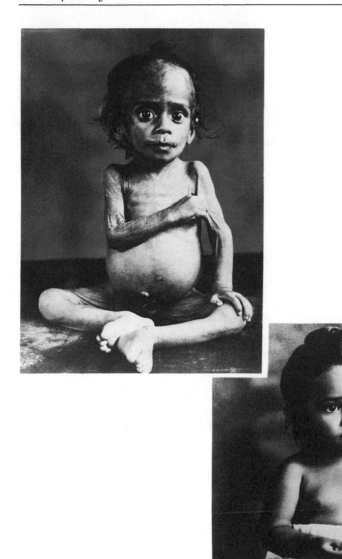

*Before and after . . . This two-year-old girl from the Andes was suffering from severe malnutrition. Within six months she was well-fed and healthy, thanks to a rehabilitation centre which taught her mother how to feed her properly. How far do you think poverty is linked with ignorance? How can the problem be tackled world-wide?*

world resources. They are the managers. It is with them, therefore, that the main responsibility for tackling world poverty lies.

The Brandt Commission pin-pointed three areas where global
action could be taken. First, the World Bank could be given the
power to encourage land reform, by giving special aid to those
countries prepared to enforce it. Secondly, an international body
could be set up to encourage industrial development in the nations of the South, as well as stable prices and a fair market for
their exports. And thirdly, the United Nations could do more to
fight the three main causes of world poverty: the arms race, high
consumption of resources, and population growth.

3. *Birth control.*   The mention of population growth raises a vital
but difficult issue. There is no doubt that the world's poverty
problems would be greatly eased if birth control was practised
more widely in the South. But many people in these countries
are against contraception on principle. And Christian opinion is
divided, too.

The Roman Catholic Church opposes the use of contraceptives. Pope John Paul II has stressed this again and again on his
world tours. According to Roman Catholic doctrine, the two main
purposes of sexual intercourse (to strengthen a couple's love-
bond and to start new life) must never be separated. Contraception drives a wedge between the two, so it is wrong.

Most other Christians disagree with the official Roman Catholic attitude to birth control. They point out that the Old Testament's command, 'Have many children' was given to man and
woman in a half-empty world. Today, the world is over-full.
Every new life is not a much-needed extra pair of hands, but an
embarrassing extra mouth to feed. God's instruction to multiply
was part of the much bigger commission he gave humanity to
manage the world in a responsible way. The majority of Christians therefore believe that they (and others) are thoroughly justified in using contraceptives to limit the size of their families,
and thus stretch the resources of an overcrowded world a little
further.

**Questions for discussion**

1. What more should the countries of the North be doing to
   alleviate poverty in the South?

2. Why do you think the level of aid is falling? Are the reasons good ones or bad?
3. How far is human greed and selfishness to blame for world poverty?
4. Do you think people in the North should lower their standard of living to identify with those in the South? If so, how?

# 21. War and peace

Imagine you are in a tight corner. You are on your way home late at night, when someone attacks you. No-one else is around. What do you do — try to hit back, or at least get a good look at your assailant's face so you can give evidence against him later if he is caught?

That certainly sounds sensible, and if your attacker is convicted and sent to jail, you may well think it is no more than he deserves. But Jesus had some different advice. 'Do not take revenge on someone who wrongs you', he said. 'If anyone slaps you on the right cheek, let him slap your left cheek too.' And he went on, 'You have heard that it was said, "Love your friends, hate your enemies." But now I tell you: love your enemies.' (*Matthew* 5:39, 43–44).

Now think yourself into a different situation. This time it is real, not imaginary. A girl in her twenties called Catherine Genovese was stabbed again and again by a man who had followed her on her way home. He took almost half an hour to kill her. She screamed for help, but no-one came. It turned out afterwards that at least 38 people had seen the murder from their windows, but not one had lifted a finger to phone the police. They just did not want to get involved.

If you had been one of those 38 witnesses, how would you have reacted? If the man was arrested, would you have offered to give evidence against him, to see that justice was done? How does Jesus' advice to 'love your enemies' fit that kind of situation, when it is not you who comes under attack, but someone else?

If you put those two examples of assault under the magnifying glass, you would cover most of the incidents which lead nations to war. Your own country may be attacked by another, in which case you may go to war in self-defence. Alternatively, some other country may be over-run by an 'international mugger', in which case you may decide to fight on its behalf, so that justice can be done and the aggressor stopped from attacking anyone else.

## Love and justice

Faced with this kind of situation, Christians are pulled two ways. Jesus' teaching on *love* makes it hard to see how killing in war can ever be right. But *justice* is an important Christian principle, too. Non-resistance allows aggressors to get away with their spoils, which is obviously unjust, and they may be ready to fight to the death to keep what they have seized by force.

Let us explore these two principles a little further.

(i) *Love seems to support pacifism.* Christians feel the strength of pacifist arguments especially strongly, because the God of the Bible is a God of love (see *1 John* 4:8), and one of Jesus' titles as Messiah is Prince of Peace (see *Isaiah* 9:6). The Old Testament describes very vividly how the Messiah is totally against war: 'He will settle disputes among the great powers near and far. They will hammer their swords into ploughs and their spears into pruning-knives. Nations will never again go to war, never prepare for battle again.' (*Micah* 4:3).

When the Messiah came, he fitted that description exactly. Jesus matched his teaching on loving enemies by the personal example he set. When Peter tried to defend him with a sword in the Garden of Gethsemane, he would not allow it (see *John* 18:10–11). A few hours later, at his trial, he told Pontius Pilate, 'My kingdom does not belong to this world; if my kingdom belonged to this world, my followers would fight.' (*John* 18:36). And after being sentenced to death, he prayed for his executioners while they were hammering nails into his hands, 'Forgive them, Father! They don't know what they are doing.' (*Luke* 23:34).

Jesus' crucifixion did not only show how far his love could be stretched. It also proved how successful a policy of non-resistance in the face of violence could be. Nearly two thousand years later, the cross is still the badge that Christians wear, and it is worn by millions all over the world.

But now we must look at the other side of the coin.

(ii) *Justice seems to support making war.* The Bible says 'God is love', but it also leaves us in no doubt about God's concern for justice. The Old Testament, in particular, describes how God can use war to put injustice to rights. He can even be described as 'a warrior' who sends his people out to fight and trains them for battle (see *Exodus* 15:3, *2 Chronicles* 6:34 and *Psalms* 144:1). And in case we dismiss that as typical Old Testament bloodthirsty warmongering, we find that the New Testament also allows for the use of force in the interests of justice (see, for example, *Romans* 13:1–5).

Jesus himself was a man of love and peace, but he did not hesitate to use force when necessary. To stop tradesmen exploiting visitors to the Temple, for example, he lashed out with a whip (see *John* 2:15). And the language he used to describe God's final judgement at the end of the world makes reports from today's war correspondents sound mild in comparison (see, for example, *Matthew* 23:29–36).

Are pacifists, then, simply people who put love before justice, and war-makers people who put justice before love? No, the picture is more complicated than that! There are times when *refusing to fight may be a denial of love*. Jesus said, 'The greatest love a person can have for his friends is to give his life for them' (*John* 15:13). That verse appears on many war memorials. Those who die in a battle to defend their country may well claim to have loved their neighbours better than many conscientious objectors who refuse to take up arms.

The opposite can also be true, because *fighting wars may be a denial of justice*. One of the greatest injustices in today's world is that while some people have more than enough to eat, others go to bed starving. It has been calculated that £17 billion would be needed each year to provide enough food, water, health, housing and education for everyone in the world. That sounds an enormous sum of money — until you realize that this is the amount the world spends on arms every two weeks. Scrap the arms race, divert the money to feed the poor, and a major injustice might be put to rights.

## Just war and nuclear pacifism

Many centuries ago, Christian thinkers worked out a 'Just War' theory to help puzzled people make up their minds about the rights and wrongs of fighting in a war. This theory tried to strike a balance between love and justice. It laid down four conditions which must be met if a war is ever to be called 'just'.

*First*, a declaration of war must be made by the government. This was to ensure that the politicians had every chance to settle a dispute by diplomacy before hostilities started. *Second*, the war must have a just cause. This ruled out conflicts which arose from national pride or empire-building. Self-defence was considered a just cause. So was the need to re-possess territory occupied by an invading army. *Third*, war must have a just aim. This was taken to mean that fighting must stop as soon as the particular wrong that had started the war was put right. The main aim must always be to restore good relationships with the enemy, not to humiliate them. *Fourth* and last, war must be waged by just means. This meant that no more force must be used than was strictly necessary to gain the war's limited goals, and that those not directly involved in the war effort must be kept out of the fighting.

These guidelines were never easy to apply, but until recently they have helped Christians to walk the tightrope between love and justice. They have also helped to shape international agreements on the conduct of war, such as the Geneva Conventions. In the last 50 years, however, the arrival of nuclear weapons and their sophisticated delivery systems has driven some people to the conclusion that the Just War theory must be abandoned.

It is certainly very hard to see how a nuclear war could ever satisfy the fourth of those Just War conditions. A United States Congress report estimates that an all-out nuclear attack against military and economic targets in the U.S.A. and U.S.S.R. would kill up to 77 per cent of the American population and up to 40 per cent of the Soviet. It is difficult to think of a cause big enough to justify that kind of slaughter, and all distinctions between combatants and non-combatants would inevitably be lost. Once the warheads were armed and the missiles on their way, babies would die just as surely as soldiers.

We now have to think about war in a new way. As the American writer Arthur Koestler puts it, 'Before the thermo-nuclear bomb, man had to live with the idea of his death as an individual: from now onwards, mankind has to live with the idea of its death as a species.'

Faced with the nuclear threat, some Christians are looking for an alternative to the Just War theory. Others — a growing number — are convinced that nuclear pacifism is the only way out, if the Christian values of love and justice are to direct our decisions. Even the threat to use nuclear weapons, they would argue, is immoral. If we intend to use them, even to retaliate, we are wrong. And if we do not intend to use them, but keep them as a deterrent, we are living a lie.

**A Christian response**

How, then, should Christians respond to the threat of war? Here
are one or two suggestions to start you thinking:

(i) *Be realistic.*   The New Testament traces international conflicts
to human nature: 'Where do all the fights and quarrels among
you come from? You want things, but you cannot have them, so
you are ready to kill; you strongly desire things, but you cannot
get them, so you quarrel and fight.' (*James* 4:1–2).
     Fighting will only end when human nature changes. That is
no doubt why Jesus forecast that the world's last days will be
marked by war, not peace (see *Mark* 13:5–13). The Christian who
thinks, 'Perhaps one day there will be no more war', is being
more optimistic than Christ.

(ii) *Be honest.*   War is an evil. All Christians believe that, whether
they are out-and-out pacifists or supporters of the Just War theory. Going to war can only ever be justified if it is a less evil
course of action than any other alternative.
     Television films sometimes make war look exciting and at-
tractive. But the glamour is only skin-deep. Christians believe it
is stupid to make war appear romantic or even to idolize its
heroes.

(iii) *Be peace-makers.*   Jesus told his followers to get involved in
world affairs — on the side of the peace-makers. 'Happy are
those who work for peace', he said, 'God will call them his
children!' (*Matthew* 5:9).
     A lot of aggression stems from suspicion and fear. Therefore
anything that encourages people to be less suspicious and afraid
of others will promote peace. That is why the Helsinki Final Act
of 1975 spoke of 'confidence-building measures' (CBMs for short).
The kind of CBMs in view were the establishment of demilitarized
zones, advance warning of military manoeuvres, exchange of
information and observers, and measures to enforce arms control
agreements. Perhaps there is room for more ordinary measures
too. What about a school trip to the Soviet Union next time,
instead of one to France or Switzerland — even if it means saving
up a little more money?

*This little Cambodian refugee, wounded and hungry, knows nothing about the political reasons behind the fighting. Who should help the civilian victims of war? Have governments a responsibility? Or must the voluntary agencies try to cope?*

**Questions for discussion**

1. Do you agree with the Christian idea of a 'just war'?
2. Does a nuclear deterrent safeguard our freedom, or threaten it?
3. Should war ever be glorified? Do soldiers deserve to be praised, or should only the horrors of war be portrayed?
4. 'Fighting is part of human nature, so there will always be wars.' How do you react to that view?

# 22. Human rights

You do not have to move far today before you hear people talking about their rights.

> 'What right have you got to do that?'
> 'I know my rights!'
> 'You've got no right to be here anyway.'
> 'I've got as much right here as you!'

Usually such 'rights talk' is heated, because we normally only talk about our rights when other people threaten to violate them. That is certainly the way the human rights issue comes across in the newspapers and on television today. We watch demonstrators marching in support of the oppressed, the exploited, the unemployed and refugees. We hear the slogans they shout, attacking those who persecute minority groups for their race, their colour, their politics or their religious opinions.

Often the issues that bring out the noisiest demonstrations are being fought out at the other end of the world, but the television screen brings them right into our living rooms. And it does not really matter whether the news item features Palestinian refugees in Lebanon, guerrilla fighters in Central America, dissidents in the Soviet Union or refugees from Afghanistan. Whenever and wherever men and women are being treated in an 'inhuman' way, there is something deep down in most of us which makes us want to take sides with oppressed people in their fight for their rights.

**What are human rights?**

What are these 'human rights' which make us so indignant when we see them ignored and abused? People have been trying to define them for centuries, and it is remarkable how closely the definitions agree. Here are just three examples from different periods of history which would not raise many eyebrows if they appeared in one of tomorrow's newspapers:

'It has appeared to us to be a very good and reasonable system not to refuse to any of our subjects, whether he be Christian or belong to any other religion, the right to follow the religion that appeals most to him.' (*The Roman Edict of Milan*, A.D. 313)

'We hold these truths to be self-evident; that all men are created equal; that they are endowed by their Creator with certain inalienable rights; that among these are life, liberty and the pursuit of happiness.' (The *American Declaration of Independence*, 1776)

'We hope for a world based on the four human freedoms. The first is freedom of word and expression . . . The second is the freedom of everyone to worship God in the manner he chooses . . . The third is freedom from want . . . The fourth is freedom from fear . . .' (President Roosevelt, 1941).

Coming a little closer to our own day, the most complete programme of human rights that has been put together, and the one to which people usually appeal first when they are oppressed, is the United Nations' *Universal Declaration of Human Rights*. This was passed by the General Assembly, meeting in Paris, on 10 December 1948. It comes in 30 different Articles, so it is too long to quote in full here, but the following is a summary of its main provisions:

— the freedom and equality of all people, whatever their race, language, sex, religion, status or political opinions;
— the right to life, liberty and security;
— equality before the law and the protection of the law;
— the right to privacy;
— the right to freedom of movement, both inside and outside one's own country;
— the right to nationality;
— the right to marry and start a family;
— the right to own property;
— freedom of thought, conscience and religion;

— the right of peaceful assembly;
— rights concerned with playing a part in the government of one's country;
— rights concerning social security, work, trade unionism, rest and leisure, standards of living, education, cultural life and social order.

## Where do rights come from?

Jacques Maritain, who was a member of the committee that drew up the U.N. *Declaration*, tells how someone expressed amazement at the way delegates were able to agree about human rights, when they disagreed violently about practically everything else. 'Yes', came the reply, 'we agree about the rights — *but on condition that no-one asks us why.'*

The question 'Why?' would have brought back almost as many answers as there were delegates! Nevertheless, it is an important question to ask. Why was it that representatives from so many different parts of the world — socialist and capitalist, developed and under-developed, Christian, Buddhist and Moslem — were able to agree on a list of human rights?

When anyone takes a stand on their 'rights', he or she is really appealing to some set of standards that no-one can question, or to some source of authority that everyone can accept. But where in the world can we find such standards? And where is this mysterious source of authority that commands such amazing, universal agreement? These questions are very old ones. Philosophers have struggled for centuries to find answers to them.

Some say it is *the law-makers* who give us our rights. The laws of the land forbid murder and stealing, so we gain from the law the right to live securely and to own property. But this is an inadequate answer. After all, our law-makers might change the rules next week, but they could not take away our rights so easily. The law can *protect* or *threaten* human rights, but it cannot either *make* them or *remove* them.

Others say it is *human reason* that underlies our agreement about human rights. Whatever our culture, religion or political views, we all have minds to reason with. So we use our brains to work out basic principles of social survival.

This is a much more persuasive answer. It does not take much brain-power, for example, to work out that in a world where people live closely together, murder and stealing must be wrong, whatever the law of the land says. We can therefore take the next logical step, and agree that security and ownership are human rights.

Christianity, however, takes us one step further. According to the Bible, human rights have their origin in *God*, not in state laws or even in human reason. 'Getting my rights' means 'being treated in the right way'. And that means 'being treated in line with God's standards of rightness'.

This is a very important difference. Christians believe it is God who provides the authority which makes sense of human rights. It is he who sets the standards. That comes out particularly strongly in the Old Testament. As the prophet Isaiah put it, 'the Lord God Almighty shows his greatness by doing what is right' (*Isaiah* 5:16; see also *Deuteronomy* 32:4 and *Psalms* 97:2).

In the New Testament, Paul accounts for *un*believers' convictions about human rights in exactly the same way. They may not believe in God, but his standards are 'written on their hearts' whether they like it or not (*Romans* 2:14–15). This is because every man and woman in the world is 'created in God's image' (*Genesis* 1:26–27). That is a fact of life which no atheist can escape. And part of what it means to bear God's image it to recognize his standards of rightness.

The Christian approach to human rights is therefore three-dimensional. I do not just respect my neighbour's rights because he is a fellow-man (that would be two-dimensional). I respect him because I am under obligation to God to give him his rights. The Old Testament story about Cain and Abel illustrates this very well. Cain tried to get out of his responsibility for his murdered brother ('Am I my brother's keeper?', he asked). But he could not evade his responsibility to God. ('The Lord said, "What have you done? Listen! Your brother's blood cries out to *me* from the ground." ' (*Genesis* 4:8–10).)

## The Christian difference

This God-centred approach does not make very much practical difference to the list of human rights that Christians accept. In 1963, Pope John XXIII produced an encyclical called *Pacem in Terris* which enthusiastically supported all the rights outlined in the United Nations *Declaration*. But putting God at the centre does alter the way Christians understand and interpret those rights. Here are four ways in which the Christian difference is seen most obviously:

(i) *The value of the individual.* In 1948, the Soviet bloc abstained when the *Universal Declaration of Human Rights* was put to the vote at the United Nations. They had very good reasons for doing so, because in Marxist teaching the rights of the individual must always be set below the interests of society. 'There should be no isolated individual', writes one communist authority, Makarenko, 'either protruding in the shape of a pimple or ground into dust on the roadway, but a member of a socialist collective.'

Christians would agree that there are times when individuals should put society's interests before their own. But the Christian gospel puts a much higher value on the individual's value than Marxism does. No Christian can say, as Caiaphas did before Jesus' trial, 'Don't you realize that it is better for you to let one man die for the people, instead of having the whole nation destroyed?' (*John* 11:50). It is the individual who bears God's image, and it is the individual for whom Christ came and died (see *Matthew* 18:12–14, *Galatians* 2:20).

Christians are not alone, of course, in stressing the value of the individual so strongly. But biblical teaching ensures Christian support for all measures which protect the right of individual citizens to appeal against decisions of their governments (as a British citizen can, for example, under the Council of Europe's *Convention on Human Rights*).

(ii) *Responsibility before rights.* When we discuss human rights today, we are usually thinking about our own. In the Bible, it is the other way round. The focus is usually on our responsibility to treat other people rightly.

The New Testament's teaching on marriage illustrates this vividly. A modern book on marriage might start by setting out the wife's rights and then (if it was fair) go on to defend the rights of the husband. Paul sets about things in a completely different way. He begins with the wife's main *responsibility* ('Wives, submit to your husbands as to the Lord'). Then he sets out the husband's main *responsibility* ('Husbands, love your wives just as Christ loved the church and gave his life for it', *Ephesians* 5:21–25). A balance is struck, but there is no whisper of rights at all. Notice the God-centred approach, too. No wonder this kind of teaching jars on modern ears!

(iii) *Rights and merits.*   A Christian's main responsibility in life is to love. 'Love the lord your God', said Jesus, 'Love your neighbour as you love yourself.' (*Mark* 12:30–31). These two love commands have been called God's 'Universal Declaration of Human Responsibility'.

As we saw in Chapter 2, Jesus made it clear that the demands of neighbour-love are unlimited. They reach out to embrace the complete stranger you meet in trouble (*Luke* 10:25–37), and even your worst enemy (*Matthew* 5:43–47; see also *Exodus* 23:4–5).

This duty to love makes an enormous difference to the Christian's outlook on human rights. Because God commands Christians to love, people in need have a right to the Christian's practical concern. They may have done nothing to deserve it. They may have done a great deal to deserve the opposite. But God's love command means that they can expect it as their right. This is why, for example, the Bible sets out generosity as a duty, not as an optional extra for nice people (see *Deuteronomy* 15:11 and *1 Timothy* 6:17–18).

(iv) *Subordination of personal rights.*   Jesus' love led him to surrender his personal rights for the sake of others. At the end of his life he was the victim of injustice, but he made no move to claim his legal rights. And he taught his disciples that the same standard was expected of them. 'If anyone wants to come with me', he told them, 'he must forget self, carry his cross, and follow me' (*Mark* 8:34). In other words, Christians are expected to accept the same violation of their personal rights as Jesus did, when love demands it.

This is not to say that a human right ceases to exist when it is surrendered. There is nothing inconsistent in Christians fighting to defend a right for other people, when they have voluntarily surrendered it in their own lives themselves (see, for example, *1 Timothy* 5:17 and *1 Corinthians* 9:1–12). Love may well demand both.

**Questions for discussion**

1. Where do human rights come from?
2. Why are human rights still abused, when there is such widespread agreement that they should be upheld?
3. Should an individual's rights ever be ignored for the sake of the majority?